Doing What's Right, Right

D1569545

Doing What's Right, Right

In the Not-for-profit Sector

Helping community organizations and
churches operate more effectively

Lindon E. Saline

D.B. Reinhart Institute for Ethics in Leadership
Viterbo University
La Crosse, Wisconsin

ISBN 10: 0-9816896-0-4
ISBN 13: 978-0-9816896-0-9

This book was previously published in 1991
in a private edition by the author.

D.B. Reinhart Institute for Ethics in Leadership
Viterbo University
900 Viterbo Drive
La Crosse, WI 54601
www.viterbo.edu/ethics

Book design and composition by Robert Schreur
Printed by Publishers ExpressPress, Ladysmith, Wisconsin

D.B. REINHART INSTITUTE for **ETHICS IN LEADERSHIP** *at* VITERBO UNIVERSITY

The D.B. Reinhart Institute for Ethics in Leadership is located on the campus of Viterbo University in La Crosse, Wisconsin. Its mission is to promote the concept of ethics in leadership as integral to the advancement of American society and to advance leadership and ethics through publications, courses, conferences, workshops, and public forums.

To my very best friends,
J.H.S. and J.C.,
and to the professional staff and volunteers
who want to serve society more effectively
through churches and community organizations

Contents

Foreword

This book is for people who feel their community organization or church could and should be more effective in fulfilling its mission. The author's premises are the following:

- The need for more effective community organizations is greater than ever.
- Many community organizations and churches are currently performing well below reasonable standards of performance.
- Meeting societal needs demands excellence in leadership and management from paid staff and volunteers in community organizations and churches.
- Many paid staff and volunteers want to perform their role as leaders, managers, and workers more effectively than they currently know how to perform.

The meaning of "reasonable standards of performance" is whatever the leaders and members decide explicitly or implicitly. The assessment may be based on intuitive "gut feelings" or on specific observations which may be either favorable or unfavorable (*e.g.*, decrease in membership, increasing attendance at events, delinquent pledges, etc.). Of course, leaders, members, and volunteers should never be complacent about an organization's performance. The goal should always be to serve society more effectively.

The purpose of this book is to help leaders, paid staff, and volunteers perform more effectively, grow professionally and spiritually, and experience pleasure and satisfaction in their serving society through their community organization and their church. The book is designed for individual or group study and is readily adaptable as source material for use in a workshop format.

The book is not scholarly in the sense of documenting references and sources of information. Rather, the leadership and management model developed here is based on my personal lifetime experiences, study, and observations. During a 36-year career with the General Electric Company, I had for more than a decade the responsibility for managerial and executive education at the General Electric Management Development Institute. Since my retirement from General Electric in 1984, 1 have been actively involved as a volunteer with a wide variety of community organizations and my church. My bias is not that community organizations and churches should be run like businesses but rather that they should be operated like community organizations and churches using sound management principles and practices salted with Christian love and guided with prayer to achieve "reasonable standards of performance."

This book is about leadership and how to make things happen (*i.e.*, doing the right things, right). The first chapter is conceptual: it is a generic discussion about exceptional leaders who must not only do the right things but also do things right. The other chapters are highly prescriptive: they deal with the nitty-gritty of what leaders and workers should do to improve organizational performance. Each organization has unique leadership needs depending on its size, age, setting, current performance, and other factors. Some of the precepts suggested here may at first seem to be over-kill or overwhelming or even inappropriate. Nevertheless, all of the precepts contain lessons and reminders even if not used formally or totally. Leaders and workers are encouraged to use whatever fits their situation, getting an idea here or there that may be helpful now or in the future. The book does not cover subject areas such as fund raising, program design, marketing, and the like. But it is directly concerned with how to lead and manage the committees and organizational components responsible for various programs and activities.

There are many "thank you's" that should be listed. However, I have not kept proper notes over the years to give credit to the authors, lectur ers, leaders from all societal sectors, bosses and co-workers, and friends who have influenced my own leadership style and the model developed here. The content is a meld of ideas and insights from all of those sources. The model, its application to local churches, and the words are totally mine except for Appendices A and B. They are respectively examples of an operational plan and committee responsibilities adapted from a functioning church. Although I played the major role in developing and writing the original documents, I have here improved, disguised, and labeled them as Fictitious Christian Church–Anywhere, USA, and have arbitrarily dated them to 1986. A variety of organizations (Chamber of Commerce; churches—particularly First Presbyterian Church, La Crosse, and Ormond Beach [Florida] Presbyterian Church; government; colleges and schools; social agencies; and businesses) have served as "test beds" for parts of this material presented in workshop format. For their patience, support, and feedback I am very grateful, indeed.

Two individuals have been especially key in this undertaking. Charles Crawford Smith, minister of the Congregational Church of New Canaan, Connecticut, challenged me in the early 80's to "help us ministers to learn how to be better managers." In my retirement from General Electric my very best friend, favorite person, and loving wife, Jane, encouraged me to write this book and graciously and kindly fed me "patience pills" to help control my energy, enthusiasm, and expectations.

Doing What's Right, Right

Chapter One

You Can Be an Exceptional Leader

What are the attributes, attitudes, and skills

that make a difference?

Exceptional leadership is doing the right things as well as doing things right. The notion of doing *the* right things embraces any effort to accomplish a goal deemed worthy by the relevant constituency. The notion of doing things right focuses on generating and using resources (human, financial, and physical) efficiently and effectively to achieve the worthy goal (the right things).

Both notions—doing right things and doing things right—are essential ingredients of exceptional leadership. To wit: we are bombarded with exhortations from politicians, church leaders, and social activists to feed the starving people of Africa, relieve the farm crisis, decrease the federal deficit, improve accessibility and affordability of health care, increase availability of student loans, eliminate nuclear power, lower interest rates, disarm unilaterally, protect our environment, reduce unemployment, and assure our freedoms. But seldom do they suggest practical means for generating and allocating resources to achieve these multiple, sometimes conflicting, and highly desirable "right things." That kind of visionary and idealistic leadership focuses on doing right things with little attention to doing things right.

Conversely, business executives, government bureaucrats, entertainers, educators, journalists and authors, chairpersons of community and

church committees, and others may be very effective and efficient in pro-
ducing cutting edge airplanes, insecticides, video recordings, radars and
navigational systems, championship athletic teams, fact-finding com-
missions, and innumerable other products, programs, and services—
presumably in response to the wants (not necessarily the needs) of people
and of organizations. Even such efficient performance does not qualify
as exceptional leadership since the end use of such products, services, and
programs may not be regarded as worthy—on balance—by many in the
relevant constituency.

Visionaries and idealists are needed to conceive and define things
that are worthwhile doing. Managers are essential to accomplishing the
worthwhile things efficiently and effectively. This book is about the un-
common person who is both the visionary and the manager. The exceptional leader is not necessarily the "top dog" in an organization. He
or she may function in various roles and with various levels of assigned
responsibilities and delegated authority.

The accolade of "exceptional" for leadership and leaders is, indeed, in
the eye of the beholder more than on an absolute and measurable scale.
Even so, there seem to be some attributes, attitudes, and skills that I have
personally observed as common to a wide variety of truly exceptional
leaders: business executives, career and elected government officials, clergy, educational administrators, researchers, teachers, health care managers, and a potpourri of church and community volunteers. Conversely,
I have also observed a lack of the same attributes, attitudes, and skills
among alleged leaders who, in my judgment, are ineffective.

The purpose of this chapter is to share and elaborate on these attributes, attitudes, and skills common to a wide variety of exceptional
leaders and lacking in others. To help the reader develop a structure for
self-assessing his or her leadership strengths and limitations, these highly
interdependent characteristics are grouped into four (admittedly arbi-
trary, but convenient) categories:

- Knowing your territory
- Using charisma
- Having well-developed values and goals
- Making things happen.

Knowing Your Territory

Exceptional leaders (in the parlance of *Music Man*) know their territory (business, church, community organization, etc.). They have an intimate knowledge of their organization or constituency, how it operates, and its policies and practices. This knowledge includes an assessment of strengths and limitations, needs and wants, available and potential resources, and by implication opportunities to make a difference by meeting needs and wants more effectively. Leaders know about organizational mission and goals and about the organization's products, services, and programs.

Effective change efforts generally start from where people and organizations are. Therefore, leaders must be familiar with the historical and current traditions, rules, and regulations defining the territory. They must be sensitive to societal trends and what's happening in the community, nation, and world and how it impacts their territory. Over a period of time exceptional leadership is manifested as changes in the territorial traditions, rules, and regulations or in organizational policies, practices, products, services, and programs. The best leaders anticipate and help shape the changing social, economic, political, and technological environment. Others may be completely oblivious to forces of change or at most only responsive to whatever is changing.

Leaders are aware and sensitive to obstacles and competitors in their territory whether they are leading local church programs, operating a major business, providing federal grants to states for health services, or teaching in a university. Competitors and obstacles are not always obvious and, in fact, may be quite subtle. Individual people or organizations who are status-quo oriented are commonplace and need to be dealt with surely but carefully. More difficult competitors to discern and to handle are enjoyable and worthwhile activities (golf *vis-à-vis* attending church), alternative ways to use financial resources (a European trip *vis-à-vis* a financial contribution to the local symphony), and conflicting use of governmental resources (tobacco price supports *vis-à-vis* "stop smoking campaigns" and cancer research). Similar examples of competitive alternatives for scarce resources (time, treasures, and talent) exist throughout our society. Leaders know that competition is part and parcel of the American fabric, and they strive to influence how we choose among the "chocolates and vanillas" that are available to us.

But what if a person doesn't know the territory? Is that person blocked from becoming a leader? The answer is an emphatic, *No!* To illustrate, consider first-term US Presidents. They have much to learn about the territory of that exalted and powerful office even if they have previously been a Governor, US Senator, or US Vice President. Leaders must always read, ask, observe, discuss, and seek counsel. Leaders learn about their territory by doing and, very importantly, assessing how they might have done better. Exceptional leaders are always learning and building on their experience and knowledge base as they seek to know more about their territory. The position helps develop the person. Less experienced potential leaders simply have a greater need and urgency for learning. Therefore, whether you are contemplating accepting the chairmanship of the Boy Scout Troop Committee or a high level government position or a church office or a new position in a business, the process for getting to know your territory is largely within your personal control. Keeping up to date and learning more about your territory as a leader is a never-ending process.

Using Charisma

Charisma as a human quality is the analog of a magnet in ferrous metallurgy: it attracts people in a seemingly magic way. Even so, charismatic people have some distinctive and discernable attributes, attitudes, and skills that can be nurtured purposefully and used creatively.

The ability to clearly articulate and breathe life into one's vision is invaluable in building charisma. Using metaphors and carefully crafted phrases is a charismatic skill that excites people, helps them glimpse the leader's vision, inspires them to develop ownership, and encourages them to participate.

- Would you prefer painting the Cass Sreet Bridge across the Mississippi River in La Crosse, Wisconsin, or refurbishing the Gateway to the West?
- Which is more likely to enlist the energy and resources of church people: a collection to support mission projects in foreign lands or One Great Hour of Sharing?
- As an engineer or scientist, would you rather work for a company that believes, "If you can dream it, you can do it," or for one that simply touts its proximity to pleasant beaches?

Charismatic people are enthusiastic, optimistic, energetic, and confident but not cocky or arrogant. They are success-oriented; failure is not in their lexicon. Nevertheless, they tend to be risk-takers (not the same as reckless gamblers), operate at the cutting-edge, dare to be different, and make thoughtful but timely decisions.

The charismatic leader is committed and persevering. Commitment is more than involvement. For example, using ham and eggs as a metaphor, the chicken is involved but the pig is committed. Follow-through and meeting performance standards and schedules in spite of unforeseen obstacles and adversities differentiate exceptional leaders from others. The exceptional leader exhibits physical, intellectual, emotional, and spiritual stamina. They believe that:

> The man who once most wisely said,
> "Be sure you're right then go ahead,"

Might well have added this, to wit:

"Be sure you're wrong, before you quit."

Charismatic people are fun to work with. They are trustful and predictable. Exceptional leaders regard leadership not in terms of power but as an opportunity for service to their co-workers and constituency. They develop individuals and build teams by serving people rather than by using them. Leaders have a low NIH (not-invented-here) factor. Everyone is important; everyone can make unique contributions; everyone can experience economic and psychic rewards. The leader understands his or her challenge is simply to help people discover and perform what they are best equipped to do. Charisma is what helps turn people on to do what needs to be done.

Having Well-developed Values and Goals

Exceptional leaders have well-developed goals and values. Although subject to modification as one has new experiences and acquires new learning, goals and values should be relatively stable if they are, in fact, to enhance the quality of leadership. Intellectual and emotional energy can then be focused more on achieving than on changing directions or on rationalizing actions and behavior. Exceptional leaders know where they are going personally in life and where they want to lead their organization. They carefully think through, develop, and share the mission, purposes, and goals of their organization. They sense very deeply the potential importance of their organization's and their personal contributions to the well-being of society. They know society will be better off if they and their organization fulfill their mission and purposes and accomplish their goals.

Leaders are productive dreamers. They have visions; they actually see, feel, hear, and experience the reality of success in their fantasies. Contrary to a common adult admonition to young people, day dreaming is essential to progress and achievement, as we are reminded in "Happy

Talk" from the musical, *South Pacific:*

> You gotta have a dream.
> If you don't have a dream,
> How you gonna have a dream come true?

Values are what we live our lives by. What we do and our relationships with others demonstrate our values more than what we say. Indeed, actions do speak louder than words. Integrity, trustworthiness, loyalty, and responsibleness are characteristics common to all exceptional leaders. They develop high and healthy self-esteem and strive for excellence in their personal and organizational performance. They always aim high; quality is their hallmark. Exceptional leaders "shoot for the stars," believing that

> Ideals are like the stars. We may never reach them, but like the mariners on the seas, we chart our courses by them.

Values are learned and assimilated from life experiences, studies, and observations. Families, friends, teachers, clergy, celebrities, fictional and real life heroes: their role-modeling, instruction, and support or disapproval of our actions influence our values for better or for worse. Exceptional leaders have deliberately thought about their values and know what they believe and support. They are not permanently rigid, but they are far from wishy-washy or situational. Leaders share their values when appropriate and are willing to be measured by them. It is not easy, but it is worthwhile, to write a private outline or essay about one's values. What are your religious, economic, political, and social tenets? What guidelines govern your behavior and relationships with your family, friends, boss, peers, and strangers? Do you obey speed laws, pay all your income tax, etc?

Making Things Happen

The late Nicholas Murray Butler, Nobel Laureate and President of Columbia University, observed that people can be divided into three groups:

- A very small and elite group that makes things happen
- A somewhat larger group that watches things happen
- The vast majority of people who don't know anything is happening.

Exceptional leaders are in the small and elite group that makes things happen. Leaders must by definition be future-oriented. They know there is no future in believing something can't be done; they know the future is in making it happen.

Making things happen generally involves working with and through other people. That's what management is about. Exceptional leaders are excellent managers. Although each has his or her distinctive style and approach to managing, there are some common elements which are described ever so briefly here and are elaborated on and applied to community organizations, churches, and the like in subsequent chapters.

Among the common elements of managing are four highly interdependent activities: planning, organizing, integrating, and measuring.

Planning (Chapter 2) is a process of analysis and synthesis that helps an organization define its mission, vision, strategies, operating objectives, and resource allocation. The appropriate degree of formality and sophistication of the process depends on the nature and size of the organization or the activity.

Organizing (Chapter 3) is a process for structuring an organization; allocating work and resources within the structure; delegating responsibility, authority, and accountability; and staffing, compensating, and developing the human resources to accomplish the desired work.

Integrating (Chapter 4) is the on-going managerial activity that facilitates organizational components and people working together effectively by sharing information, resolving conflicts, reducing undesirable duplication, coaching and motivating, and re-assigning (when necessary) responsibility, authority, accountability, and resources. The leader, as integrator, builds synergy within the organization so that $1 + 1 > 2$.

Measuring (Chapter 5) is the on-going managerial activity that reviews performance and progress against planned objectives and resource (financial, human, facility, materials) utilization against resource budgets. The leader, as measurer, is not being distrustful of the organization or people. Rather, measuring is the servant leader's means for discovering where additional help and resources may be needed, encouraging and coaching people, and expressing appreciation for a job well-done.

The effectiveness of the four interdependent managerial activities may well be determined in the long run by the quality of three kinds of managerial communications (Chapter 6):

- Interpersonal or one-on-one
- Organizational
- External.

The exceptional leader uses knowledge of territory, charisma, and well-developed goals and values to communicate effectively. Timeliness, openness, and verified clarity are marks of effective two-way communications. Planning and conducting efficient and worthwhile meetings (Chapter 7) are essential skills of exceptional leaders.

Exceptional leaders also manage their personal time effectively, and they respect the time of the people they are leading. They manage their time to enable them to live balanced lives—physically, intellectually, emotionally, and spiritually. Exceptional leaders are whole people, quite unlike the workaholic octogenarian who ruefully observed that his epitaph should accurately read, "Born a human being; died a bill collector." Exceptional leaders frequently are the "busy people" who can take on one more task for their church, community, or employer. That is because they manage themselves (including their precious time resource) as effectively as they lead others.

Self-assessment

Getting things done through the process and results of managing (planning, organizing, integrating, and measuring) can be an invaluable means for learning about your personal leadership characteristics. The managing process can give you a feeling for how well you know your territory, how effectively you use your charisma, and whether your values and goals are developed as well as you might like. The inter-relatedness of all the leadership characteristics will become even more evident in subsequent chapters. However, you may want to ask yourself:

- What are my leadership strengths and limitations?
- What do I already know that I can start doing now to be a more effective leader?
- What should I try to learn from this book or other sources to improve my leadership attributes, attitudes, and skills?

It's Not All Glory

Exceptional leaders generally experience great personal satisfaction from their personal and organization's contributions to society. But that does not mean they are loved and admired by all people. They must also be prepared to be envied, chastised, disliked, and ridiculed. Many people choose to be dedicated and committed followers. They appreciate and look for competent, enthusiastic, creative, energetic, and successful leaders. Others prefer to be neither leaders nor followers: they simply take life as it comes and are more or less content with whatever happens as long as they don't have to unduly exert themselves. Still a few others seem to be born obstructionists or wish to be anointed as leaders but have been unable or, perhaps more likely, unwilling, to develop the qualities they need to be exceptional leaders.

The latter group tends to find many excuses for disagreeing, complaining, and not performing to agreed-upon standards and milestones. Frequently they are status-quo people who abhor and fight change even when change is clearly needed. They are uncomfortable in facing and attempting to resolve conflict. They tend to value being personally liked more than doing responsibly what's right for the organization. Some approaches to dealing with conflict are suggested in Chapter 6.

Exceptional leaders would, of course, like to be liked. They do not relish encounters with those who almost habitually obstruct or impede progress. Neither do they ignore or avoid such situations. Rather, exceptional leaders are patient, sensitive, careful listeners, persistent, steady, persuasive, and appropriately flexible. Generally the organization will eventually follow exceptional leadership. If not, perhaps the leadership was incorrectly perceived as exceptional.

So What?

You may already be an exceptional leader in your family, church, place of employment, profession, community, government, or wherever. If so, you are a valuable asset to our society. Keep up the good work by doing right things and doing them right.

If you want to improve your leadership capabilities, that option is open to you. Leaders are not necessarily born as leaders. Leaders work diligently and purposefully—sometimes consciously, sometimes unconsciously—to develop and use leadership attributes, attitudes, and skills.

Papers, books, and workshops focusing on leadership abound and are available to you at local libraries, colleges, or professional societies. Choose an outstanding leader known to you, analyze his or her strengths, and emulate them. Very importantly, get involved in leadership roles where you can practice being an exceptional leader. Then, take time for self-evaluation and reflection. You will surely grow as a leader and be personally well-rewarded for your leadership efforts.

Planning
for Performance

How to Determine the "Right Things to Do"

for Your Organization

The very word "planning" is anathema for many people in their personal lives, employment, community, church, and volunteer activities. People who avoid planning rationalize that planning takes time away from doing, that the future is unknown anyway, and that they are simply too busy to plan. It is important to remember that "not-to-plan" is in itself one way to plan: that kind of organizational adhocracy probably does not know where it is going or how it is going to get there. Those "avoid-planning-at-whatever-cost" people and organizations are probably those who would benefit most from thoughtful planning. Indeed, the efficacy of the maxim, "Plan your work and, then, work your plan," has been demonstrated time and time again. A unit of time properly invested in planning can save many units of time later, assure efficient use of human, financial, and other resources, and enhance organizational performance.

What Planning Is

Planning is a process of analysis and synthesis that helps an organization define its mission, vision, strategies, operating objectives, and resource allocation. The purpose of planning is to determine what to do and how to do it effectively. Planning is future oriented. The appropriate planning horizon might be one day, one month, a year or two or twenty, depending on the organization and the nature of the specific activity (*e.g.*, long-range plan, an event, major capital campaign).

The planning process combines research, forecasting, analysis, and synthesis to produce the plan. Ideally, all aspects of the planning process should be documented so the basic information and data bases, "thinking," alternatives considered, and decisions can be shared and communicated. Even so, the best planning document is a loose-leaf binder that can be easily modified in response to or in anticipation of changing planning inputs. Plans should never be "chipped in granite." With whatever degree of sophistication and formality planning is implemented, there are common elements that comprise the planning process which are shown in process relationship to each other in Figure 2.1:

1 Developing a mission
2 Listing stakeholders
3 Assessing the organization
4 Analyzing and forecasting the environment
5 Delineating stakeholder needs and wants
6 Developing a vision
7 Synthesizing possible organizational thrusts and activities
8 Developing potential resources
9 Selecting strategic directions and operational activities
10 Documenting the plan
11 Developing "what if" trigger points and contingency plans.

The process can be adapted to meet the specific needs of any organization or committee or project. The process can be used by a board of directors during a planning retreat (perhaps a day or two) or a planning session (perhaps two or three hours) or by an individual project leader in a private work session. The process serves as a discipline for generating and reviewing pertinent information and asking and answering critical questions. This is not a book of answers,

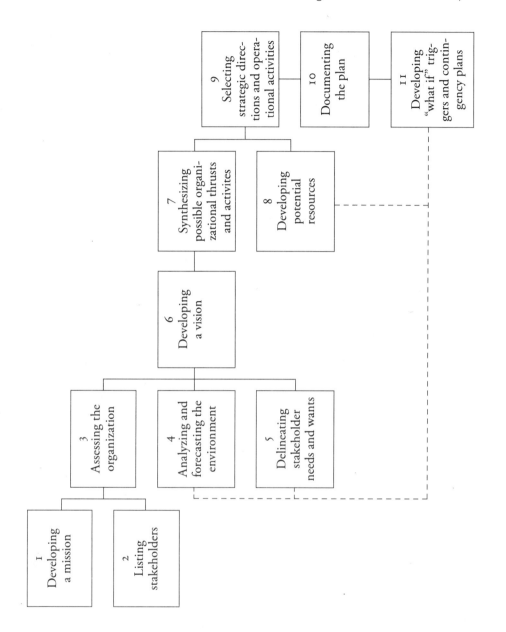

Figure 2.1 A Planning Process

Each of the eleven planning elements is discussed in the above listed numerical order even though the planning process, *per se*, is iterative. The process has been used effectively in whole or in part in businesses, government, educational institutions, churches, cultural organizations, and social agencies. Examples of each planning element are referenced to Appendix A which is a thoroughly documented plan for a fictitious church set in an arbitrarily selected time frame (1986). A church was chosen for the example and teaching vehicle because churches are familiar to many people and churches are more complex than most community organizations.

Developing a Mission

An organization's mission is a unique statement of its purpose, affiliation (if any), operational approach, hallmarks of performance, and constraints and restrictions. The mission statement should be brief. It should provide directional focus while having sufficient breadth to accommodate, anticipate, and respond to changing societal factors. The Preamble to the US Constitution is an excellent example of a mission statement. It has provided for two centuries directional focus and flexibility for how the American people collectively want to live their lives. (See Appendix A, p. 66 for an example of a local church mission statement.)

Developing a mission statement can be an exciting learning experience since it usually stimulates thoughtful introspection and vigorous discussion. Leaders frequently have different and unspoken ideas about what the organization has been doing and, even more importantly, what the organization should be focusing on in the future. Without a common acceptance and understanding of the mission to serve as a basic premise for planning, an organization's leaders can spend many unproductive hours arguing about what to do, how to do it, and allocation of resource.

Listing Stakeholders

Stakeholders are individuals or organizations who will be impacted by and have a deep interest in what your organization does and how successfully it performs. Stakeholders may be generic groups or specific entities. For example, a church might list its stakeholders as:

- Members
- Youth, elderly, homeless
- "x" nursing and care center
- Senior minister
- Synod, presbytery, conference, or diocese
- "y" college
- Churches "a," "b," "c"
- Local media
- Community residents
- Local social agencies
- Foreign mission "d."

The possibilities are numerous. Therefore, constructing the list to meet the needs of the specific organization requires careful thought. Using a sports contest metaphor, your stakeholders are the players, opponents, coaches, spectators, trainers, referees, sports reporters, concessionaires, and the like. Knowing your stakeholders is essential to knowing your territory. Not knowing them is unnecessarily assigning yourself a handicap.

Assessing the Organization

Assessment requires a careful review of the organization's strengths and limitations. The review should cover as broad a range of subject areas as the leaders can conceive, including:

- Brief history of organization with highlights
- How the organization has performed against goals
- Reputation and image
- Quality and relevance of programs and services
- Relationships with members
- Relationships with other organizations

- Relationships with the community
- Membership growth or shrinkage
- Status of human, financial, and physical resources.

Assessment should ideally be based on inputs from various points of view internal and external to the organization. Stakeholders can make important contributions to the assessment. The means for obtaining such inputs include individual and group interviews, surveys, analysis of records, informal conversations, and comparisons with other organizations. Without knowing how an organization is currently doing, it is virtually impossible to conceive of changes to enhance future performance. The assessment exercise can also be counted on to stimulate profound discussion among the organization's leaders. (See Appendix A, p. 68.)

Analyzing and Forecasting the Environment

Change in the environment is inevitable due to social, political, economic, technological, and competitive factors. Organizations gain or lose in progressing towards fulfilling their mission according to their anticipation and responsiveness to the forces of change. Change can influence an organization positively or negatively. A disruptive obstacle to one organization may well be a golden opportunity for another.

The variety of change forces are mind-boggling. Here are only a few examples that might influence a local church:

- Increased chemical dependency
- Merging of major church organizations
- Growth of over-65 population
- Swing towards conservatism in government
- Movement towards world-wide markets and competition
- Greater public interest in deficits, inflation, taxes
- Reductions in federal support of local social programs
- Increased interest and effort in biblical exegesis
- More competition from recreational activities and hobbies for

time of church leaders, workers, and members
• Availability and pervasiveness of communications technology.

The challenge is to discover and anticipate forces of change, analyze them as to their positive or negative potential, and devise ways for creatively using or handling them. There are many ways for discovering and evaluating change, such as through the media, by attending lectures or participating in discussion and study groups, or by consulting with "think tanks" and so-called futurists. However you tackle the environmental assessment and forecast, you should focus on your specific organization, mission, and geographic location. Environmental change factors seldom operate with equal force and impact in all situations. (See Appendix A, pp. 69–70.)

Delineating Stakeholder Needs and Wants

What do your stakeholders need from your organization? What might they want? Need suggests "minimally acceptable" whereas want suggests "hopes."

For example, for a specific church, the members as stakeholders may need only adherence to doctrine in worship and teaching and the most basic pastoral services. On the other hand the members as stakeholders might also want excellent preaching, a quality music program, and a creative and vigorous local mission program. A church employee as a stakeholder needs a fair wage, safe working conditions, and employment stability, but to the extent possible wants challenging and interesting work, a health care program, opportunity for growth and advancement, vacation, and a compatible supervisor and peers.

Delineating stakeholder needs and wants encourages leaders to develop a variety of ways for fulfilling an organization's mission. The needs and wants of stakeholders "A" and "B" might conflict or they might be congruent. For example, a specific church might find that elderly members want an elevator whereas young parents place a high priority on a full-time director of education. Conflicts and congruencies of stakeholders' needs and wants are important flags for leaders. We are reminded that nowhere is it suggested that life would be a cakewalk!

Developing a Vision

As mentioned in Chapter 1, exceptional leaders have a vision of what they want their organization to become. Throughout the planning process an organization's leaders should be developing a vision for the local church and "fine tune it" through discussion with each other. An example of a vision for a local church is given in Appendix A (p. 71).

Synthesizing Possible Thrusts and Activities for the Organization

Creating an array of possible activities and thrusts is a synthesizing process that combines the assessment, environmental analysis and forecast, and stakeholder needs and wants within the framework of the organization's mission statement. The possible organization activities may simply be more of what is already being done and therefore quite familiar; new, "off-the-wall" ideas that initially sound preposterous; or approaches that other organizations conceived and implemented successfully.

These "possibles" may be specific activities such as a new program (*e.g.*, church bell choir) or a new service (*e.g.*, recordings for shut-ins) or a broad long-term thrust (*e.g.*, increase financial support of world-wide missions). The synthesizing process should release as much creative energy as possible to answer the question, "What might the organization do to fulfill its mission more effectively?" The creative process should not be constrained by criteria such as feasibility or doability. The more "possibles" generated the better.

Developing Potential Resources

Organizations use financial, human, physical, and information resources in the implementation of their programs. Except in starting a new organization these resources are available in some amount. Even in starting a new organization, startup resources are frequently available (foundations, government, etc.). When already available resources are thought to be insufficient, additional resources can be purchased, collected from donors, borrowed, recruited, or copied.

Many (perhaps even most) organizations unduly constrain their creative and expansive thinking about possible thrusts and activities by limiting their vision of potential resources. If a possible activity or thrust holds enough potential for meeting the needs or wants of an organization's stakeholders, then mustering resources to implement that activity becomes a planning challenge and opportunity in itself. The resource challenge, then, is for the organization's leaders to document carefully the resources already available, how the available resources might be reallocated for new activities, and the available possible ways of acquiring additional resources. The resource challenge should be addressed in an action mode.

Selecting Strategic Directions and Operational Activities

Strategic directions are the broad statements that provide focus, areas of emphasis, and guidance for an organization over a period of years. Operational activities are very specific and pertain to what the church will do during the next year or so. Strategic directions and operational activities should, of course, be mutually supporting and consistent and fit within the framework of the organization's mission.

For a local church, a strategic direction might be to increase mission financial support over a five year period from 15% to 25% of the church's annual operating budget with particular emphasis on local mission activities. (See Appendix A, pp. 72–73.) A supportive operational activity for the church could be to establish and operate an emergency food center. Whereas a local church might develop only three or four strategic direction statements (see Appendix A, pp. 72–73), it is likely to have twenty to fifty operational activities. (See Appendix A, pp. 74-85.)

The challenge for the organization's leaders is to sort out "possibles" (activities and thrusts) and to tentatively prioritize them based on criteria such as:

- Appropriateness based on the mission and the size and nature of the organization
- Relevance to stakeholder needs (which must be fulfilled if the organization is to survive) and wants (which should be at least partially met if the organization is to thrive and distinguish itself)
- Doability considering the kinds and amount of resources required
- Criticality:
  - essential for an organization's survival
  - necessary for organizational vitality
  - desirable for organizational distinction.

The selection and prioritization process for developing strategic directions and operational activities is, of course, iterative, since the resources (financial, human, physical, information) available may be limited even though potential sources have been thoroughly explored. After allocating resources for the essential activities, the leaders must make trade-offs among the necessary and desirable activities. Strategic directions will also evolve during the selection and prioritization process.

Considerable judgment, flexibility, and creativity are necessary since the organization leaders' vision may have been too narrow or too broad relative to "possibles" and to potential resources. It is helpful to look on planning as a learning process or an exploratory and discovery process whereby the leaders arrive at a "final" organization plan through a series of successive approximations. Even then, the "final" plan should not be "chipped in granite."

Documenting the Plan

Documenting the selected strategic directions, operational activities, and resource allocation is a prerequisite for communicating and implementing the plan. The members of the organization, the workers, and the organization's staff deserve to know what the organization's leaders have on the action agenda in the coming year and beyond. Acceptance and understanding of the plan by those stakeholders is essential for harnessing their involvement and support.

Documentation for financial resources is commonly called a budget. The line item budget (see Appendix A, p. 87) is most familiar. Income and expenditures can be as finely detailed as the organization desires, and the line items, in turn, can be grouped in various ways. Although useful for accounting and internal control, the line item budget is less useful for communicating to stakeholders. Narrative program budgets (see Appendix A, p. 86) are more useful and meaningful for that purpose.

A narrative program budget consists of a statement or two describing each major program (group of commonly focused activities) and the resources allocated to the program. The financial resources allocated to the program include planned direct expenditures as well as an estimate of indirect and overhead costs.

For example: The church mission program will be given new emphasis in the next five years as we increase mission financial support from 15% to 25% of our operational budget. Next year the mission resources will increase from $42,800 to $49,500 and consist of the following items:

Staff	$7,700
Use of building	3,200
Teaching and promotional materials	800
Local programs	10,500 (*currently* $3,200)
World-wide missions	27,300
TOTAL	$49,500

In addition, the Mission and Social Action Committee will require four additional volunteer workers to develop and administer the expanded mission program.

Budget documentation should include more than current financial requirements. Also important are capital budgets for the next five years or more and the human, physical, and information resources to implement the planned activities. The form of documentation will vary widely depending on the size and nature of the organization. Frequently organizations neglect to consider resource needs other than finances and/or they do not bother to document them. That is why there is often a last minute scramble to recruit chairpersons and committee members.

Budgets should also delineate sources of income. Developing and assuring the productivity of the income sources should itself be an essential activity. The success of the funding activity depends in many ways on the quality and success of the organization's current and past programs and services. Success in the programs and services areas begets success in fund raising and in generating other resources. People like to join and support winning teams.

Documenting the selected operational activities for an organization should include specific and measurable objectives and milestones for each of them. (See Appendix A, pp. 74–85.) The details and content of the documentation (objectives, milestones, allocated resources) should be worked out jointly by the supervisor and the activity leader.

There are three kinds of measurable objectives:

- *Absolute:* Conduct four adult workshops on subjects A, B, C, D.
- *Judgmental:* Enhance the appearance of the church grounds and parking lot as seen by the Chairman of the Grounds Committee.
- *Stochastic:* Maintain a music program evaluated as 8.0 or greater on a scale of 1.0 to 10.0 by 90% of a random sample per month.

Milestones for each activity should be explicit:

- Complete task X no later than 12/10/88.

Without explicit and agreed-to objectives and milestones there is grave danger of misunderstanding of who is to do what by when. Leaders at all levels in the organization need careful documentation to constructively do their integrating and measuring work as discussed in Chapters

4 and 5. Workers need the documentation if they are to be secure in their personal work performance and if they are to be team players. An organization's members need the documentation so they can support the organization's program with their resources (time, treasures, and talents).

What If

Planning for an organization is in the context of an ever-changing societal environment. It is future-oriented and therefore is based on many assumptions. What if the societal assumptions are grossly inaccurate? What if implementation does not proceed as scheduled? What if income is greater than planned or if more people volunteer to become workers? What if capital fund pledges lag or key paid staff leave for other jobs? There are innumerable "what ifs" that should be at least partially thought through and considered before they happen. An organization's leaders are well-advised to outline alternative critical actions to cope with the potentially most damaging "what ifs." (See Appendix A, p. 75, Objective B&G–7.)

Indicators of potential danger or favorable windfalls can be listed as flags for leaders as they do their integrating and measuring work. Leaders and workers can then re-assess the situation and determine whether specific operational plans should be modified before a situation gets out of control and/or cannot be rescued.

Chapter Three

Organizing
for Performance

How to Help People Work Effectively

in Fulfilling the Organization's Mission

Organizing is a process for structuring an organization; allocating work within the structure; delegating responsibility, authority, and accountability; and staffing, compensating, and developing the human resources necessary to accomplish the desired work.

Community organizations and churches are organizationally structured in accordance with by-laws. The structural components generally include a governing body (council, board, session), officers (chairperson of board, president, vice president, secretary, treasurer), sometimes a paid staff (executive director, minister, office staff), and an array of committees. One church structure is shown schematically in Figure 3.1; committee responsibilities for that structure are given in Appendix B (p. 89). How the organization functions—that is, who does what—may be described, of course, with varying degrees of formality, completeness, and accuracy or may even be undocumented and simply agreed-to in discussion. The structure should be flexible enough to adapt to the strategic directions and operational plans. That is, the plan should determine the structure rather than (as is frequently the case in government) the structure determine the plan.

In any case the chairperson, president, or minister should function as the "chief executive officer" or "general manager" and be responsible and

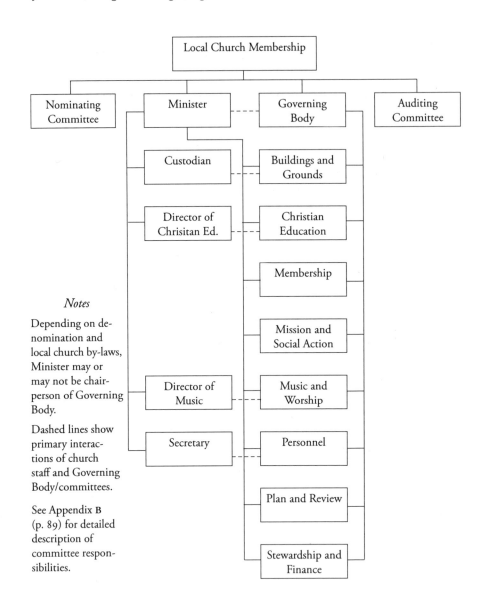

Figure 3.1 A Local Church Structure

accountable for providing and/or assuring overall leadership (vision and management). In that role the leader does not do all the work but rather energizes the properly staffed (paid and volunteer) organizational components to perform the work authorized by the governing body and documented in the strategic and operational plans. General management is an essential but not a forte and favorite activity of many ministers, social agency directors, and cultural leaders, which highlights the critical need for developing and using an organization structure that can effectively support the leaders in carrying out their general management work. Creative use of the organizing process is a prerequisite for developing an effective support system to meet that need. Organizational leaders, of course, have a responsibility to use the structure, the paid staff, and volunteers to help perform and fulfill their general management work and responsibilities. In the illustrative church organization structure the Plan and Review Committee (Figure 3.1 and Appendix B, pp. 99-100) can be very helpful to that end.

Developing an Organization Structure

The starting point for developing or improving an organization structure is to know the existing structure. How effective has it been? What are its strengths and weaknesses? Are the weaknesses structural (*i.e.,* inconsistent with the work to be done) or staffing (*i.e.,* unqualified, disinterested, or ineffective people)?

Structure should always follow strategy (or planning). What work needs to be accomplished to fulfill the plan? Can the work to be done (on-going and new or additional work) be given appropriate emphasis in the existing structure? Should new components be established or existing components eliminated or modified? Whatever the structure and however the components are named should "make sense" to the organization's leaders, staff, volunteers, and membership.

The structure, of course, needs to be staffed. Will the financial resources of the church permit the addition of paid staff? Will qualified and interested members volunteer to fill new committee chairs and do the necessary committee work? If structure cannot be staffed, it is then necessary to consider alternative structures or even make changes in plans and strategies.

Documenting the Structure

The development of the organization structure is based on the work to be accomplished within each component and must be consistent with the organization's by-laws and its rules. Documenting what that work is and how it can be accomplished is very helpful in assuring the proper functioning of the structure. (See Appendix B, pp. 91-103 for documentation of the church structure shown in Figure 3.1.)

The documentation for each component should include:

- Responsibilities
    - the area of focus
    - specific on-going tasks
    - staff relationships
    - planning
    - resource management
- Authority
    - commitment of expenditures within approved budget
    - approval for payment of bills
    - development and implementation of planned programs
    - any specific withheld authority
- Accountability
    - resource management
    - fulfillment of approved programs
    - integration with staff and other components
    - relationships
    - timely and informative reports
    - quality of participation in planning

The structural documentation should be reviewed and modified (if appropriate) annually so that it is consistent with and supportive of strategies and plans. The structural documentation is essential to the work of the paid staff (if any), volunteers, and nominating committee.

Staffing

Staffing is the greatest leverage factor in assuring effective organization operation. Creative and aggressive plans and a well-thought-through organization structure are for naught if the staffing—paid and volunteer—is poorly executed.

The starting point for staffing is to determine the work that must be performed for each position. That determination can be made by analyzing the strategies, plans, and organization structure. What are the qualities needed to perform the paid and volunteer leadership work in each position (education, experience, knowledge, attitudes, energy, values, skills)? Is the position to be filled for an indeterminate period (*e.g.*, a minister or board chairperson, executive director) or for one to three years (*e.g.*, a volunteer committee chairperson)? If the position is on the governing body, what qualifications are needed to "round-out" and give "balance" to the governing body? Generally too little effort is given to specifying what is needed for specific positions. When that is, in fact, the situation, the quality of staffing and the performance of the organization suffer in the long run.

When the specifications for open positions are completed, the lists of potential candidates should be prepared and carefully reviewed. It is not good for either the organization or the individual to fill a position with an unqualified individual. Dedication, friendliness, and popularity are not sufficient criteria for potential candidates. Members should not be on the potential list for leadership positions unless they are also qualified (knowledge, skills, etc.) and willing to devote the time to do the work required in a specific leadership position. And let us be forthright: being an effective community organization or church leader requires considerable time. Being on the governing board or a committee chair should not simply be considered an honorary position.

Potential candidates for volunteer positions should be approached in a serious and unhurried manner as to their interest in being part of the leadership of an organization. A five-step procedure is ideal but can easily be adapted to fit specific situations.

Step 1. Invite all potential volunteer candidates (self-selected or committee selected) to an information meeting designed to inform them about the organization plans and structure, the specifications for open positions, and the time commitment to fulfill the open positions.

Step 2. Conduct the information meeting as outlined in Step 1. Encourage and inspire them. Urge them to carefully consider the available opportunities to serve the organization. Have them indicate their specific interests at the meeting or within a few days following this meeting.

Step 3. Follow through to determine the specific interests of potential candidates. Match candidate interests and qualifications with openings. Select candidates to be nominated, and confirm with candidates. Notify and thank potential candidates who will not be nominated at this time and enlist their commitment for committee or other work. The organization should strive to "include" rather than "exclude" all who desire to serve. Committee workers are always needed.

Step 4. Present and nominate candidates for election in accordance with the by-laws.

Step 5. Conduct training sessions for the newly elected leaders and provide for the transition from the "old" to the "new" leaders.

Compensation Policy

Staff employees are, of course, compensated for the work they perform. Unfortunately, the basis for compensation in community organizations and churches is sometimes mysterious or willy-nilly.

Compensation might include wages and salaries; special allowances for housing, car, and education; vacation, sick, and personal time; health insurance; pension and social security; and other related elements. Although compensation, *per se*, is not a long-term motivator, perceived inadequate compensation can be a de-motivator. The tendency in many churches and community organizations is to treat employees (particularly ministers and other professional staff) as super-spiritual beings who can somehow survive on being paid well below what run-of-the-mill human beings require.

There have been many excellent compensation systems developed over the years. Rather than review them here, the basic process for determining appropriate compensation for employees is presented and can be adapted to fit the specific organization.

1. Evaluate each job in terms of responsibilities assigned, performance expectations, and needed qualifications.
2. Determine the "going rate" (total compensation) for similar positions in the community.
3. Set a position rate for each job. All elements of compensation should be considered. The position rate is the compensation paid for fully adequate performance on a sustained basis.
4. Compare the position rates for all paid positions in the organization and adjust them so they make sense in relationship to each other.
5. Calculate a position range for each position. The starting level (bottom of range) may be 20% less than the position rate; the ultimate level (top of range) may be 20% above the position rate. (The *starting level* would be paid to an individual who is

inexperienced but otherwise qualified; the *position rate* is paid to someone who consistently performs fully satisfactorily; the *ultimate rate* is paid to an individual who demonstrates unusual initiative and exceptional performance—quality, quantity timeliness, attitudes—on a sustained basis.)

6. Movement from the starting level to position rate should require at most three to six years. If longer, then the individual is probably not suited for the position and termination should be considered. When an employee moves to the ultimate level, the sustained exceptional performance suggests a need or opportunity to restructure, assign more responsibilities, and determine a new position range for compensation.

7. Adjustments in compensation should be based on performance as measured against work plans and goals developed jointly among the employee, the supervisor (*e.g.*, the minister or executive director should supervise the paid staff), and the cognizant board or committee. Work plans should be explicit and measurable (absolute, judgmental, stochastic as described in Chapter 2) and have milestones. Performance evaluations should be conducted periodically by the supervisor and board or committee, not only as a basis for compensation review, but also to support the employee's performance. Employee performance reviews should be documented and signed to assure there is common understanding (even if not complete agreement).

8. Depending on inflationary and other forces, position ranges should be reviewed periodically and adjusted as appropriate. Adjustments in compensation for changes in position range should be explicitly differentiated from changes in compensation for performance for each employee. Employees should be informed of the salary policy and the specific dollars for the position range for their specific job.

Developing and Training an Organization's Staff and Volunteers

The work of the organization is performed by people. Some are full-time or part-time employees; most are volunteers. Even though they are motivated spiritually or otherwise in some measure towards serving the organization, they all benefit personally and perform more effectively when they are involved in a program of personal and professional development and training. Such programs include four primary elements.

Work

> The work assignment, *per se*, is potentially the major source of professional development. Careful work planning is critical for performance as well as professional development. Opportunity should be available for the worker to be creative in how to perform the work more effectively and to be expansive in what is done. Expansiveness or enlarging the job does not imply unilateral decisions by the worker to not do the assigned work, but rather to demonstrate that more can be done. Doing real work in a variety of roles builds a broad base of know-how and experience for paid and volunteer workers that is essential for the continuing growth and vitality of the organization.

Coaching

> The growth of an organization's leaders and workers is facilitated by coaching. Coaches explain fundamentals, role model to some extent, observe performance, give feedback, suggest alternative approaches, answer questions, and offer support and encouragement. Supervisors (*e.g.*, executive director, minister) are responsible for coaching their employees and volunteers but others (*e.g.*, committee chairs) can be helpful in coaching as well. Coaching is also an important aspect of a manager's integrating and measuring work as discussed

in Chapters 4 and 5. Coaching should not be confused with doing; that is the function of the paid and volunteer leaders and workers.

Education

The right kind of education at the right time, blended with work assignments and coaching, can greatly accelerate the professional development and enhance the performance of paid and volunteer leaders and workers. The modes of education are diverse and include formal classes for academic credit, workshops and seminars at conferences, correspondence courses, reading books and periodicals, self-study via audio or video recordings, or one-on-one with subject experts. Any learning can be fun and enjoyable. Learning for professional development, however, should be directed towards improving performance on the current job and preparing for future jobs. Financial and time resources should be allocated for education for paid and volunteer leaders and workers. Frequently workshops or retreats can be designed and conducted by the paid or volunteer staff for very low cost. Excellent teaching and learning materials are readily available. Magazines received by the paid staff contain thoughtful and comprehensive articles that would be helpful to volunteers and can be made available simply by routing them appropriately.

Career Planning

Most community organizations and churches do little if anything to encourage career planning for either their paid or volunteer staff. Career planning as a process helps individuals think through their strengths, limitations, likes and dislikes, interests, values, and goals. On the basis of that kind of analysis and other factors (potential open positions, mobility, job performance, etc.), a person can deliberately choose professional job actions (work assignments, coaching, education) to prepare for and move towards his or her career objectives. Career planning is a win-win for both the organization and the paid or volunteer worker. The organization thereby can help assure a "pipe line" of more qualified volunteers to fill future open positions; motivate and encourage paid staff to prepare for more challenging jobs; and perform more effectively (even if they eventually move out of their current organization to serve elsewhere). Career planning is not a once-in-a-lifetime exercise. Rather, it should be done periodically to account for societal and organizational changes and individual growth. The goal of each career planning exercise should be an answer to the organization's leaders' and workers' question: "What professional development actions should I take next if I am to move towards my goals (as I perceive them now) for serving the organization more effectively?"

Chapter Four

Integrating for Performance

How to Keep in Touch
As a Basis for Assuring That $1+1>2$

Integrating is the on-going managerial activity of chairpersons, ministers, executive directors, committee chairs, and others that facilitates organization leaders, volunteers, and committees working together effectively by sharing information, resolving conflicts, reducing undesirable duplication, coaching and motivating, and re-assigning (when necessary) responsibility, authority, accountability, and resources.

The leader/general manager of the organization is the overall integrator. Each of the paid staff and volunteer leaders also have important integrating roles in their assigned areas of responsibility. Integrators must know what should be going on as well as what is actually going on. They keep in touch; they develop trust so they will be informed of both good and bad news; they function as helpful servant and coach in support of all the workers.

Keeping in touch with all the volunteer leaders and paid staff in an active organization is not easy. The leaders must make a deliberate effort to seek information and progress reports from the paid staff, committee chairs, *et al.,* by phone calls, in informal conversation after meetings or special events, or at specially arranged one-on-one meetings. The leaders as integrators also receive requests for guidance or assistance from volunteers in similar ways. Formal means for keeping in touch are regu-

41

lar written reports, copies of minutes or correspondence, attendance at committee meetings, and regularly scheduled staff and governing board meetings. Formal and informal means for keeping in touch are equally important. How to conduct effective meetings is discussed subsequently in Chapter 7.

The integrator mentally compares what is actually going on with what should be going on and then relaxes knowing all is well or takes appropriate action to get things on track. Hopefully there is sufficient trust (see Chapter 6) between paid and volunteer staff and the integrator so there are no major surprises or disasters but at worst only small deviations from plans that can easily be corrected or unforeseen obstacles that can be compensated for. The integrator might suggest alternate approaches, joint work with other committees, or adjustment of plans, responsibilities, and resources. Support, commendation, and encouragement are used by the integrator in a coaching mode to help motivate the paid and volunteer staff to grow professionally and perform more effectively. The leaders, general manager, and committee chairs function in their role as integrator to build synergy within the local organization or church or within its committees or activities so that $1 + 1 > 2$.

Chapter Five

Measuring
for Performance

How an Organization's Leaders Can Know

When Paid Staff and Volunteers Need Help

in Doing Their Assigned Work

Measuring is the ongoing managerial activity that reviews performance and milestone progress against planned organizational objectives and resource utilization against resource budgets.

As previously described in Planning for Performance (Chapter 2), work plans for the organization and for its committees should be documented as measurable objectives and milestones. (See Appendix A, pp. 74–85.) Resource budgets document what resources (financial, human, physical) are allocated to implement the work plans. (See Appendix A, p. 86.)

Paid and volunteer workers need to be measured regularly and to be aware how their work is progressing. Measuring is not a sign that a leader is distrustful but rather that the leader is caring and responsible. Exceptional organizational leaders want their paid and volunteer workers to succeed and, as servant leaders, they want to be helpful in whatever way is appropriate.

Measuring is a complementary activity to integrating. The two go hand-in-hand since formal and informal measuring are essential inputs for effective integrating. Keeping-in-touch as described in Integrating for

Performance (Chapter 4) is the means for informal measuring. Formal measuring is generally accomplished through regularly scheduled written or oral reports from the leaders to the governing body or to the membership.

Written financial reports should be presented monthly in a standard format. Line item expenditures and sources of income for the month and year-to-date are compared with the financial budget. Many organizations establish monthly budgets as one-twelfth of the annual budget. A better approach is to estimate seasonal expenditures and income in establishing monthly budgets, since that provides a better basis for comparing actuals when monthly expenses and income are highly variable.

At a minimum, formal financial and activity status should be reported to the governing body and other leaders. In addition, consideration should also be given to the feasibility and appropriateness of reporting monthly or quarterly—at least in summary form—to the organization's membership. It is important that the members be aware of performance trends both favorable and unfavorable in order to develop and maintain their sense of involvement and ownership. The report of the auditors should be presented to the governing board annually.

Chapter Six

Communicating
for Performance

*How Leaders Can Enhance Their Capability
for Working With and Through Other People
to Accomplish the Work of the Organization*

The work of fulfilling the organization's mission depends ultimately on people who are dedicated towards serving the organization. They work in concert to plan and meet specific objectives and milestones consistent with the strategic directions and operational plans determined by the organization's leaders. Working in concert demands excellence in communications among paid and volunteer workers and leaders and with the membership. Such excellence in communications is too seldom found, and the performance of the organization suffers accordingly.

Some Basics of Excellent Communication

Communications is a broad term that includes a variety of people-related processes for conveying, receiving, and exchanging information, feelings, ideas, knowledge, directions, confirmations and denials, and support. A simple but instructive communications model (Figure 6.1) consists of three primary elements: transmitters, receivers, and modulators. The model lists the wide variety of operational modes for the three elements.

In the communications model there is a transmitted message and a received message, which, it is important to note, probably differs from

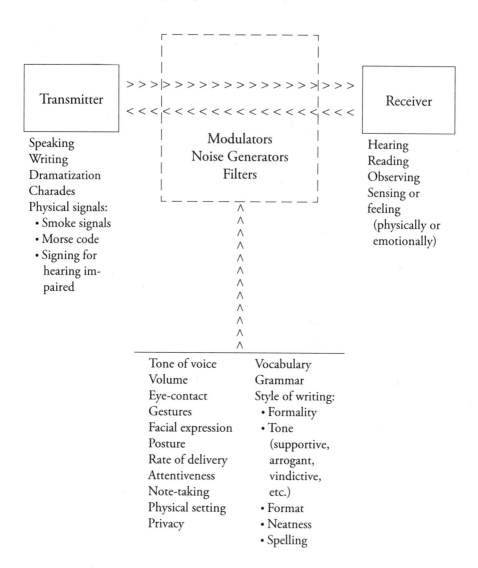

Figure 6.1: A Basic Communications Model

the transmitted message. The difference in the transmitted and received messages depends on the quality of the transmitter and the receiver and on the modulator interference. For example:

- When a person as transmitter is talking face-to-face with another person as receiver, the quality of the transmission is impacted 7% by the chosen words, 38% by the voice, and 55% by the facial expression.
- People generally speak 12 to 175 words per minute but can hear at the rate of 600 words per minute. Is it any wonder that the adult attention span is only 45 seconds? Listening, which is hearing carefully and thoughtfully, requires active concentration by the listener. Hence the need and importance for the speaker to use non-verbals to reduce the listener's mind excursions.
- *Time* magazine is said to be written for comprehension by 7th and 8th graders (if they have interest in the subject matter).

Communications effectiveness is measured by:

- The commonality of understanding achieved between people in their roles as transmitters and receivers
- Achieving desired action-oriented behavior and achieving understanding (not necessarily agreement) of the receiver for a call to action
- Impact on public and self-esteem of the transmitter and receiver
- Preserving or enhancing the basis for productive, future relationships (win the battle but lose the war).

Rather than make a few general statements about communications in organizations, two illustrations of communications in a church congregation are presented. Churches are more complex than most community organizations. Therefore, the reader can translate these illustrations to other organizations.

Communications Within the Church Worship Service

The quality and style of communications at the worship service impacts the congregation and sets the tone for relationships among the church members. The greeters (if any), bulletin, words of welcome, announcements of activities, the reading of the liturgy, the children's sermon, the choir music and hymn singing, the preaching, the praying, and the post service social time all meld to give the worshipers a feeling about the vitality and friendliness of the church. People who have moved geographically or who have had occasion to do "church shopping" within a denomination or among denominations have experienced a wide variety of church ambiences. Church leaders have responsibility for determining what kind of church ambience is desired and for implementing actions to achieve it. Such actions may be as minor as initiating a brief greet-your-neighbor period at some point during the church service or as major as changing ministers if the minister cannot perform in the manner necessary for creating the desired ambience.

Communications Within the Church Structure and Organization

Communications among church workers and leaders within the church structure and operations is less visible than at worship services but is perhaps of equal or greater importance. Exceptional church leaders must be excellent communicators in order to share their visions for the church and manage and interact with the paid staff and volunteers effectively.

Ministers are generally more effective as preachers and teachers (communicating to a group) or as counselors (one-on-one) than they are as managers (planning, organizing, integrating, measuring) which requires somewhat unique communications skills. In their role as managers, ministers frequently shy away from directing, measuring, scnsing and resolving conflicts, questioning staff and volunteers about progress, and reprimanding when appropriate, since they may feel insecure or "un-

Christian" when those actions are necessary. Governing boards can be helpful to the minister if the minister and board agree to assigning part of the follow-up responsibility and authority to a qualified volunteer. (See Plan and Review Committee Figure 3.1 and Appendix B, pp. 99-100.) In using that approach there is a danger of resentment growing if the committee chairs or paid staff are uncooperative with the assigned volunteer or if the minister feels threatened. In any case, the minister must constantly strive to improve his or her capabilities as a manager-communicator and must use that capability consistently and with sensitivity.

Local churches to be effective must be open and trustful among the components that comprise the church structure and among the paid and volunteer church leaders and workers. When communications are not open and trustful, there is danger of schisms developing within the church, burnout and frustration of leaders and workers, and a "giving up" that leads to apathy and atrophy. Conflict within a church and among church leaders and workers is inevitable. If the church tradition is to suppress or deny conflict, long term problems are likely to develop. If conflict is open, explored in love and service, and resolved, the church moves forward towards fulfilling its mission. When properly managed by excellent church leaders, conflict can, indeed, be healthy.

There is a disease rampant in many churches called NOTMA (NObody Tells Me Anything). This disease causes certain committees or cliques to carry out their church work as if they were independent entities. NOTMA can be arrested or even cured if church leaders and workers are willing to face up to it and give it their attention. The effectiveness of the cure depends on the willingness of those stricken or affected by NOTMA to share their needs for, their wants for, and their feelings about information relevant to church operations. Paid and volunteer church leaders should ask:

- Who needs to know what to help the church operate effectively?
- Who would be motivated if they knew certain information?
- Who will be turned-off by not knowing certain information?

- What information is definitely confidential?

The task is not all that easy to accomplish.

Building Interpersonal Relationships

Sharing information with and cooperation among leaders, paid staff, and workers is based on what people know or feel about each other. Their knowledge and feelings are comprised of facts, perceptions, experiences, and hearsay. Their knowledge and feelings grow positively—that is, people enhance their interpersonal relationships—when they have common values, interests, and understand each other's goals; when they have compatible personalities; and when they have mutual trust and respect.

One model for understanding the basis for a two-person (you and I) relationship is known as the Johari Window* (see Figure 6.2). Solid lines A and B in the model divide the "you and I" knowledge square into four sectors:

- *Common knowledge* is knowledge about me that each of us knows. This common knowledge is the cornerstone of our relationship.
- *My blind spot* is knowledge about me known to you but not to me. For example, you may know that my high energy level and expectations cause people to avoid working on church projects with me.
- *Unknown* is knowledge about me that is unknown to both of us. For example, I may be harboring an undiscovered cancer or the Board may be planning to ask me to chair a committee.
- *My façade* is knowledge about me that is known to me but is unknown to you. For example, I may be writing a book about leadership.

---

*I have been exposed to the Johari Window (a psychological tool created by Joseph Luft and Harry Ingham in 1955) in a variety of workshops. See Joseph Luft, *Group Processes: An Introduction to Group Dynamics* (3rd ed., Mayfield Publishing Co., 1984). Joe and Harry deserve thanks for the original idea, but they should not be held accountable for my interpretation.

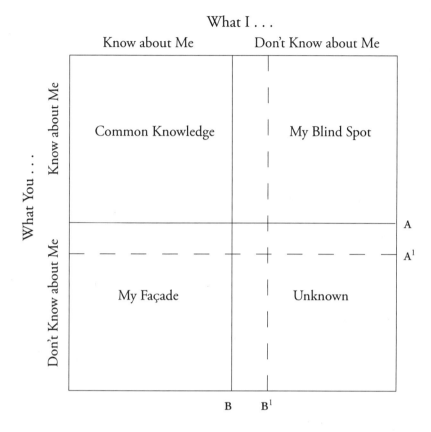

Figure 6.2: The Johari Window

The underlying premise for the Johari Window is that increasing the common knowledge sector enhances the potential for building a productive, sharing, and trustful relationship. There are two ways to increase the common knowledge sector:

- I can share with you some additional knowledge about me but previously unknown to you. Schematically I move solid line A to dashed line A¹ in Figure 6.2.
- You can share with me some knowledge about me known to you but previously unknown to me. Schematically you move solid line B to dashed line B¹ in Figure 6.2.

As we "open our windows" of common knowledge, the basis of our relationship grows consistent with our level of comfort. Our windows are opened to leaders and workers by deliberately offering and asking for information, working on projects with those who we don't know very well, taking time to get acquainted with "unknowns" at various events, and sharing, testing, and verifying perceptions and feelings bi-laterally within the comfort level of "you and me." Building relationships is not easy, but it can be done. It is certainly most appropriate for leaders and workers in churches and community organizations.

How to Deal with Ineffective Communications

Leaders and workers may need special attention and help if they are poor communicators. The ineffectiveness may be caused by poor skills in speaking, writing, listening, observing, sensing, reading, or untimely response. Ineffectiveness may also stem from poor interpersonal relationships as previously discussed. There are some guidelines that leaders and workers can use unilaterally to ameliorate those situations:

- Seek out the poor communicator. Ask for the information you need, explain how it will be helpful in fulfilling your role, and mutually determine how to handle in the future.
- In concert with the difficult communicator, set specific times and modes for exchanging information.
- As receiver, feed back in your words what you heard from the transmitter. Ask for feedback from the receiver when you are the transmitter.
- Share copies of letters and ask others to reciprocate when appropriate.
- Take advantage of *ad hoc* meetings to facilitate communications.
- Use the telephone. Leave calls. Return phone calls made to you.
- Read your mail promptly. Read between the lines for under-

standing. Ask for clarification when necessary. Respond to requests promptly.

- Share your feelings. Ask others how they feel about the quality of communications. Acknowledge that you are aware of his or her feelings. How would they like to handle in future?

Other Kinds of Communications Deserve Attention, Too

How to write newsletters, prepare speeches and presentations, and construct posters is outside the scope of this book. Nevertheless, those and many other communications skills should be nurtured and used to operate an organization effectively. There are, of course, many books, workshops, and self-study audio and video recordings to help develop a broad range of communications skills (writing, reading, listening, speaking, and improving interpersonal relationships). Leaders and workers are encouraged to use them in their professional development as previously discussed.

Chapter Seven

Conducting Meetings for Performance

How Leaders and Attendees
Can Make Meetings Worthwhile

Meetings of membership, governing boards, and committees are essential for the functioning of an organization. Still, meetings seem to be anathema to leaders and workers. Meetings are looked upon as a "necessary evil," poked fun at, and even detested.

Why? Because many (if not most) meetings are poorly organized and conducted and the attendees are ill-prepared and do not participate effectively. Meeting conveners and invitees must share the responsibility for making a meeting worthwhile.

Organizing a Meeting

Organization by-laws generally mandate that some meetings be called at specified times for specific purposes such as membership meetings to elect officers, hear reports, approve budgets, or change by-laws. Meetings of the governing boards are usually required monthly or quarterly. Committees generally meet monthly, but may be omitted depending on the committee's work and the season of the year. The chairperson or head of the component having the meeting has the major responsibility for developing the meeting agenda. If an agenda cannot be developed, obviously there is no reason for calling the meeting.

Whether the agenda is formally published or not depends on the nature of the meeting. In any circumstance, the agenda (even on "the back of an envelope") should contain at least the following items:

- Meeting place, starting time, estimated finishing time
- Purpose and nature of meeting (*e.g.,* regular monthly meeting, special meeting to consider_____, joint meeting with_____in order to____)
- Proposed order of business
  - welcome and introductions
  - opening prayer (when appropriate)
  - approval of previous minutes
  - routine reports
  - financial status
  - staff reports
  - committee reports, including progress reports against operational objectives

    Note: List who is responsible for reporting; state time allocated for each report as a guide to presenter; allow time for Q&A and discussion.
  - specific carry-over items from prior meetings
  - new business
  - introspective evaluation by group (not necessarily every meeting)
  - comments from chair
  - set next meeting
  - closing prayer (when appropriate)
  - adjournment.

In developing the agenda the chair should, if appropriate, consult with the people who will be presenting reports about the time allocated to the report so the presenter can be properly prepared.

Announcing a Meeting

To the extent possible, meetings should be scheduled at regular times. For example, the governing board might meet monthly on the third Tuesday, Committee X on the second Wednesday, and the membership on the fourth Wednesday of January and September. Some organizations hold all committee meetings on the same evening and have a common social time to facilitate the development of community and exchange of information.

Meeting announcements should be made publicly as far in advance as feasible. By-laws commonly require membership meetings to be announced (purpose, place, time) at a regular meeting in advance as well as in the monthly newsletter. Governing board and committee meetings should be listed in advance in all organization publications.

Governing board and committee meeting announcements should also be handed to or sent to the home of their members and other invitees well in advance of the meeting. That announcement should include the proposed agenda as previously discussed and pertinent back-up materials (previous minutes, written reports, new proposals, etc.). It is helpful to include as part of the transmittal letter a list of regular members as well as invited guests.

Members should be reminded to RSVP—perhaps only if they are not planning to attend. If appropriate, those not planning to attend should delegate their reporting responsibility to some other member or provide a written report. Non-attendees should also be encouraged to express their feelings about agenda items to be discussed to the extent feasible.

Members who are planning to attend the meeting have a responsibility to carefully review the agenda and back-up material. That kind of pre-meeting preparation contributes greatly to the productivity of the meeting and the quality of the decisions made there.

Conducting a Meeting

Most meetings take place in the church or organization building or offices, although retreats, workshops, planning meetings, and the like are sometimes held elsewhere to emphasize their special purpose. Wherever the meeting is scheduled, careful attention should be given to the setting and room arrangement. To the extent possible, the participants should be facing each other to facilitate effective communications. A circle or open U is more desirable than a long narrow table or row-style auditorium. The chairperson should be in direct view of all participants.

Start the meeting on time. Setting the precedent and practice of punctuality is not only efficient but courteous. Waiting for late-comers is wasteful of the time of those who are punctual. That is probably one reason why many organization leaders and workers are not enamored with meetings.

Some organization by-laws stipulate that meetings should be conducted according to *Robert's Rules of Order.* In practice that would be destructive for most church and community organizations whose meetings should follow an agenda, but the procedures should be as informal as possible. Efficiency should be sacrificed for a reasonable degree of courtesy, collegiality, and good humor. The chair should encourage and assure that all attendees have an opportunity to ask questions, hear and understand answers, and express opinions.

The chair should strive to build consensus (perhaps 80% or more agreement) on matters of organization policy and practices (*e.g.,* termination of a paid staff person or deviating from a long-standing tradition). On most matters a simple majority rule is probably appropriate. If consensus cannot be reached on matters of policy and practice, the meeting should consider postponement of any action and request additional information and further deliberation.

In conducting the meeting the chair has a responsibility for seeking closure on all items considered. Closure is manifested in various ways:

- Report is accepted, a request is approved, etc.
- The chair assigns and the assignee accepts responsibility for a specific action to be accomplished by a specific date.
- An item is carried over to a future meeting in order to provide more information, develop and evaluate additional alternatives, review with and enlist support of other groups, etc.; responsibility must be assigned and accepted by assignee.
- An item is dropped with no further consideration.

The chair is also responsible for encouraging and allowing new business to be considered. Hopefully there are no major surprises, but flexibility is necessary. Some items of new business may require immediate attention; others may be presented as an advance notice that some specific work is underway with a request for agenda time to present and discuss it at a future meeting.

"How Are We Doing?"

Many boards and committees do not take time to ask themselves: "How are we doing? How might we improve? What do others think of our work?" That kind of introspection is risky but essential for operating a healthy and vigorous organization. The chair should lead such reviews periodically. Answers to those kinds of questions will vary greatly from person to person and will not always be pleasant to the ear. If the answers are contemplated seriously and if appropriate corrective action is taken or affirmation and encouragement derived, the board or committee will emerge stronger.

The chair as leader of the board or committee also has the obvious responsibility to lead. That implies the leader's sharing at frequent intervals his or her appraisal of progress or lack thereof, vision, the challenges and opportunities, and evaluated alternative courses of action. Chairs should actively lead their charges through word and action. Being a parliamentarian is not sufficient. As a leader, are you ahead of your charges or are you running to catch up? Active and exceptional leadership is essential for fulfilling an organization's mission and modifying that mission when appropriate.

Meeting Minutes

Organizations should keep minutes of their proceedings for historical records and for facilitating operations and communications. A secretary or clerk may be elected or appointed to function as minute-taker consistent with by-laws and traditions.

Minutes should be accurate and informative and, of course, as brief as possible. They should:

- List attendees and absentees.
- List each item considered, the nature and sense of the related discussion, the specific closure, and responsibility for action.
- Record schedule and place for next meeting.

The minutes should be formatted for easy reading and comprehension and should be distributed in a timely way to members of the group, the paid staff, and others as appropriate. The chair should inform absentees if they have been assigned special responsibilities and verify their understanding and acceptance.

Responsibilities of Meeting Attendees

Responsibilities of leaders and workers as meeting attendees may be so obvious that they are known "without saying." However, when they are "without saying," they frequently are "without doing." Hence, leaders and workers should:

- Read and respond to meeting announcements.
- Call if unable to attend.
- Prepare for the meeting by:

    –fulfilling their responsibilities for specific actions

    –preparing concise, informative written or oral reports

    –reading the minutes of previous meetings.

- Be on time.
- Participate actively in the meeting by listening, questioning, and offering their opinions and suggestions.
- Avoid side-bar conversations which disturb others and distract their attention.

An Example of a Church Operational Plan

1986–87 *Operational Plans*
Fictitious Christian Church—Anywhere, USA
Prepared by The Governing Board
Local C. Leader, *Chairperson*

With deep faith and humility, the Governing Body asks God's guidance in seeking direction for Fictitious Christian Church (FCC) and in visualizing what FCC should become. The Governing Body is mindful that:

> Many are the plans in the mind of a man, but it is the purpose
> of the Lord that will be established.
>
> *Proverbs* 19: 21 (RSV)

Contents

Statement of Mission
A Brief History
Self-assessment
The Future Environment
A Vision
Strategic Directions
Operational Objectives
Resource Needs
Appendices
  How Fictitious Christian Church Is Organized (see Appendix B)
  Governing Body and Committee Members (not included here)
  FCC Organizations (not included here)

*Made available to congregation for information and discussion on
October 5, 1986.*

Statement of Mission
Fictitious Christian Church—Anywhere, USA

The mission of Fictitious Christian Church, a particular church in the United Fictitious Christian Churches of America (UFCCA) is to:

- Nurture its members in the Christian faith
- Help its members, individually and collectively, live their lives and serve their neighbors after the manner of Jesus Christ
- Tell the good news of Jesus Christ and His saving grace in the Anywhere area and throughout the world.

The order of authority for governing FCC will be:

- God, as revealed in Jesus Christ
- The Holy Scriptures
- The Book of Confessions
- The Rules and Regulations of UFCCA
- The By-laws of FCC
- The Governing Body (elected by and representing the individual members of FCC).

A Brief History
Fictitious Christian Church—Anywhere, USA

As Fictitious Christian Church approaches its 100th anniversary, it is well for us to recall our heritage. Calendar years and pastoral leadership provide benchmarks for a sample of events in the evolving life of the congregation.

1891–1916, Rev. Edwin Overmann, *organizing pastor*
Our church was organized May 22, 1891 by 43 people. Met in Presbyterian Church sanctuary on Sunday afternoons for two years before building current social room. Sanctuary added in 1905. Sponsored Miss Preach T. Gospel (member of FCC) as missionary to Mexico.

1916–1918, Rev. Harry Chanpler
Shortly after installation as Pastor of FCC, Mr. Chanpler was called into the US Army as chaplain; killed in battle on October 31, 1918. Chanpler Hall named in his memory.

1918–1933, Rev. Frank Dawn
A period of vigorous growth in membership and in physical facilities. FCC served community needs for spiritual and material sustenance during onslaught of the Great Depression.

1933–1956, Rev. Ronald Tullee
A young and dynamic minister who built on the vigorous program of the Dawn era. Even during depression and World War II the church membership nearly doubled in size, the facilities were modernized, new organ donated anonymously, and education, music, and worship program broadened to respond to new and evolving needs of community. Church staff included full-time associate minister and/or director of education at various times.

1956–1964, Rev. Ed Carger
Vigorous church program continued until 1961 when Anywhere was traumatized by a series of natural and economic disasters. The tornado, flood, and severe winter on top of the massive plant closings resulted in 35% unemployment, countless mortgage foreclosures, and a departure of people that decreased the population by 20% in an eighteen-month period. FCC responded nobly but its financial resources were severely strained.

1964–1976, Rev. Katherine Beetty
FCC pioneered by calling the first woman as pastor in the Anywhere area. Her community outreach and deep faith helped FCC members and others develop new self-esteem and hope. Anywhere and FCC had changed remarkably. Attention was also given to the maintenance of the neglected facilities. FCC was now a smaller church with only 450 members.

1976–, Rev. Current Preacher
FCC is solid in its worship program and is giving new emphasis to its local social action. FCC's Governing Body is working diligently under the leadership of Mr. Preacher to fulfill FCC's mission more completely.

FCC has made an unusually significant impact on the Anywhere community in good times and in bad. The challenge now is to anticipate and respond to the future needs of our members and the community, remembering that we are able to continue making progress in fulfilling our mission today because of those faithful servants—pastors, staff, members of the past. Thanks be to God!

Self-assessment
Fictitious Christian Church—Anywhere, USA

As FCC approaches its 100th year, the Governing Body character-izes FCC as enjoying an "aura of comfort" and being "secure, stable, and self-satisfied." The membership, relatively constant at approximately 440, is skewed towards the "over 40's." Typically 180 people participate in Sunday activities. The scarcity of younger families is reflected in the small church school and confirmation classes. Fewer than 2% of the new families moving into Anywhere are Fictitious Christians. Even so, FCC is blessed with some unique strengths and very favorable resources:

- Friendly, talented, resourceful, caring people
- Outstanding music and preaching
- Excellent pastoral services
- Beautiful and functional physical facilities, used extensively by church and community groups
- Creative church school—nursery through adult
- Active special focus groups:
    - Fictitious Christian Women
    - Youth
    - The Olders and Wisers
    - Adult fellowship
    - Members involved in community service and in the UFCCA polity.

The 1986 operational budget for FCC is $145,678 (15% greater than 1983). Pledges per pledging unit have increased from $322 (1983) to $542 (1986). Since 1983, missions and benevolences (local, national, world-wide) have been allocated approximately 17% of the annual operational expenditures. FCC has the spiritual, human, and financial resources to move vigorously as new and expanded program elements are conceived and designed to fulfill its mission. A vision for FCC and specific plans for moving towards that vision are outlined subsequently.

The Future Environment
Fictitious Christian Church—Anywhere, USA

Fictitious Christian Church operates in an ever-changing social, economic, political, and technological world. Some changes are positive; others are negative relative to their impact on Fictitious Christian Church's fulfilling its mission. What a blessing that God's love and promises are un-changing!

Here are some un-prioritized change factors that have influenced the development of the FCC plans for 1986–87:

1. Changing church structures and relationships:
   - Decreasing membership
   - Crises in many churches in 50-mile radius of Anywhere
   - Impending union of several Lutheran churches; recent merger of Presbyterian Church (USA)
   - The swing towards fundamentalism
   - Growing ecumenicity
   - Concepts of service, growth, roles, success for churches.
2. There is an increasing awareness and recognition of the diverse factors impacting on individual and family stress, including family structure (single parents, working couples), interdenominational marriages, alcohol and chemical dependency, life style, technology, passage from high school to work or college, under-developed spiritual and personal values.
3. Increasing (almost instantaneous) awareness of major societal issues, such as farm crisis, prayer in schools, peace, nuclear technology, terrorism, homeless, abused, environment, teenage pregnancy, pornography, abortion, etc.
4. Emerging Anywhere, USA area issues:
   - General population is living longer and growing older; FCC membership is growing older.
   - Increasing minority population in Anywhere, USA.

- Major employers are tending to decrease levels of employment (ABC, Inc., Campus College, Healthful Hospital).
- Renewed talk about charging churches for municipal services (water, sewerage, etc.).
- Rumor of new plant with 750 additional jobs.

5. Financial responsibility for social programs moving from Federal and State governments to communities tends to increase local taxes and need for non-governmental agencies and churches to "do more" to serve those with special burdens.

6. Increasingly distractive to church members are competitive activities such as TV, recreation, travel, two-house families, school activities and competitive sports, other worthy volunteer activities, community music activities, lottery, hobbies, etc.

7. The "one-hour-on-Sunday-morning" syndrome impacts negatively on member involvement, sharing, closeness, building a church community, etc.

A Vision
Fictitious Christian Church—Anywhere, USA

Where there is no vision, the people perish.
Proverbs 29: 18 (KJV)

The potential for FCC is limited only by the depth of its commitment to its mission, the vision of its leadership, and the faith of its members. FCC will be continually challenging itself to be visionary, creative, and entrepreneurial in using its considerable human and financial resources in the fulfillment of its mission.

The FCC will be a joyful community of Christian servants: worshipping, praying, learning, growing, forgiving, sharing, caring, working, and living after the manner of Jesus Christ. In preaching, teaching, and living the Good News of Jesus Christ, FCC will attract and nurture a growing number of people of all ages, races, ethnic origins, sexual preference, and economic status who want to explore and develop a relationship with the Trinitarian God: Father, Son, and Holy Spirit.

As a manifestation of its servant ministry, FCC will be regarded as:

- A major asset in and a vital contributor to the general well-being of the Anywhere, USA area
- An enthusiastic advocate of and contributor to world-wide missions
- A model for and a supporter of other churches and organizations in the UFCCA polity
- A thoughtful participant in the ecumenical movement.

FCC will be alert to the changing world in which it serves and to the unknown tasks that God may, in His infinite wisdom, call on it to undertake. All glory and praise be to God!

Strategic Directions
Fictitious Christian Church—Anywhere, USA

Strategic Direction 1. The essence of Christian leadership is the servant style. As servants of the Lord, we must perform better than satisfactorily. Therefore, the leaders, staff, and members will strive for excellence in the planning and implementation of all activities to fulfill the FCC mission.

Strategic Direction 2. Focus more attention and resources towards local mission and social action. Increase the proportion of the operational budget allocated to total mission and social action to at least the amounts listed in the following table:

Fictitious Christian Church Support
of Mission and Social Action

Year	($000)	% operational budget	% total budget
1980	$16.80	18.6%	12.5%
1981	16.60	21.5	19.1
1982	24.17	24.5	24.1
1983	18.90	17.5	17.1
1984	21.52	17.0	14.6
1985	22.04	17.4	16.4
1986 (est)	23.45	16.1	16.1
1987		20.0	
1988		22.5	
1989		25.0	

Note: Total budget is operational and capital.

Strategic Direction 3. Work diligently to involve many more FCC members (in addition to current leadership) in the worship and work at FCC. Pledging of personal time and talent may well be more critical than simply pledging financial resources. Special attention should be given to involving youth, communicants, new members, inactive members, and retirees.

In addition to the traditional on-going work in Governing Body Committees, there are numerous "one-time" projects that would benefit from participation from those who do not feel they can make longer-term commitments (*e.g.*, office help, coffee hour hosts, facilities maintenance, child care, etc.).

Strategic Direction 4. There will be at least one major new activity or project conceived and designed for implementation no later than July 1, 1987. It should be so significant that it will spiritually excite the FCC membership and others (currently inactive members, potential new members, the Anywhere community, the UFCCA polity).

1986–87 *Operational Objectives*
Fictitious Christian Church—Anywhere, USA

The mission of Fictitious Christian Church is fulfilled by the members working with and through the staff, Governing Body, committees, officers, and organizations listed in the Appendices.

The work consists of three categories of tasks. The first category includes most of the church's work: the traditional, on-going, absolutely essential tasks which are performed conscientiously and effectively by dedicated members in servant-fashion without any particular fanfare. A second category of tasks is special in the sense that they are expanded or new or otherwise needing of special emphasis consistent with the strategic directions. A third category of tasks focuses on the work of church leadership (vision and management) as it strives to help FCC members fulfill the FCC mission.

Although the first category of tasks has been reviewed with the appropriate and responsible FCC entity, the specific objectives for these tasks are not listed here. Progress in performing these very important on-going tasks will be reported periodically and monitored appropriately. The objectives for the second and third categories of tasks are listed here with specific milestones and measures for monitoring progress towards their completion.

Each task is assigned a number and the responsible committee or Governing Body is designated by initials:

B&G	Buildings and Grounds
CE	Christian Education
GB	Governing Body
Mem	Membership
M&SA	Mission and Social Action
M&W	Music and Worship
Per	Personnel
P&R	Plan and Review
S&F	Stewardship and Finance

The work of the Nominating Committee and the Auditing Committee is shown under Governing Body and Stewardship and Finance respectively.

Buildings and Grounds

B&G–1   Develop a master plan for expanding parking area and preserving or enhancing related landscaping.
   Start 10/1/86. Complete 2/1/87.

B&G–2   Repair stucco and paint educational wing.
   Receive bids 5/1/87. Complete 7/1/87.

B&G–3   Landscape north side of church.
   Complete 10/1/86.

B&G–4   Paint tool shed.
   Complete 7/1/87.

B&G–5   Improve boiler efficiency per recommendations of Anywhere Heating Co.
   Receive bids 9/1/86. Complete 11/1/86.

B&G–6   Paint and install false ceilings in main restrooms.
   Bids 10/1/86. Complete 12/1/86.

B&G–7   Develop contingency plan for coping with irreparable boiler breakdown.
   Complete emergency operating plan 10/1/86.
   Present estimate of replacement cost 10/1/86.

B&G–8   Repair churchyard fence with volunteer crew.
   Complete initial effort 10/1/86.
   Annual maintenance in 1987 and beyond.

B&G–9   Re-roof and insulate ceiling of educational wing.
   Bids 7/1/90. Complete 7/1/91.

B&G–10   Improve handicapped access to all floor levels of church.
   Initiate study 10/1/90. Recommendations 5/1/91.

Christian Education

CE–1   Develop and implement a graded church school program:

1986–87. Planning in process.

Implement 9/7/86 through 5/17/87.

Evaluate 12/31/86 and 2/28/87.

1987–88. Initiate special study to evaluate feasibility of bilingual church school for Hispanics.

Start 10/1/86.

Recommendation 2/1/87.

Initiate general CE study and planning 11/1/86.

Select theme and curriculum 2/28/87.

Recruit teachers 5/31/87.

Implement 9/13/87 through 5/15/88.

Rally Day 9/13/87

Advent 11/29/87

Lent 2/21/88

Evaluate 12/31/87 and 2/28/88.

1988–89. Initiate study and planning 11/1/87.

CE–2   Develop and implement Confirmation Education Program:

1986–87. Planning in process.

Retreat for participants and parents 10/86.

Confirmation Service 4/5/87.

Evaluate 12/31/86 and 3/31/87.

1987–88.

Initiate study and planning 2/1/87.

Recommend program 5/1/87.

Implement program 10/87.

CE–3   Develop and implement youth program. Work in concert with Music and Worship Committee on objectives M&W–1, 2, 3, and 6 and on special programs for Christmas, Easter, etc.

1986–87. Planning in process.

Implement 9/86.

Evaluate 12/31/86 and 2/28/87.

1987–88. Initiate special study to determine feasibility of expanding youth program beyond FCC members to include:

   • Youth from single parent homes
   • Hispanic youth
   • Joint programs with other churches
   • Christian Youth Program for grades 3–6

Initiate study 10/1/86.

Recommend actions for inclusion in 86–87 program as soon as possible but no later than 2/1/87.

Initiate general study and planning 10/1/86.

Recommend program 4/1/87.

Implement 9/1/87.

Evaluate 12/31/87.

CE–4   Develop and implement adult Sunday morning education program.

1986–87. Planning in process to focus on:
   • Bible study
   • Intensive biblically-based study of major issue (*e.g.*, nuclear disarmament, abortion, etc.)
   • Community and family issues (*e.g.*, poverty, family abuse, drugs, etc.)

Publish and distribute brochure 9/1/86.

Implement 9/14/86 through 5/17/87.

Evaluate 12/31/86 and 2/28/87.

1987–88. Initiate planning, including how to reach out to include those not members of FCC 2/1/87.

Recommend program 4/1/87.

Implement 9/20/87 through 5/15/88.

CE–5   Develop and implement special summer educational activities such as vacation church school, camps, church school picnic, retreat, etc.

Initiate study for 1987 program 11/1/86.

Recommend program 3/1/87.

CE–6   Develop and implement Leadership Workshops and Retreats in concert with Nominating Committee and Plan and Review Committee (see GB–3 and P&R–4).

Governing Body

GB–1   Appoint a task force to develop means for increasing coopera-
tive activities with The Close-by Fictitious Christian Church.
>   Appoint task force 11/1/86.
>   Recommendations 4/1/87.

GB-2   Appoint a task force to do the initial conceptual and planning
work for a major year-long celebration in 1991 to commemorate
the 100th anniversary of the founding of FCC.
>   Appoint 100th Anniversary Task Force 3/1/87.
>   Develop vision, theme, and guidelines.
>>   Receive inputs from committees, organizations, staff,
and congregation 5/1/87 to 9/1/87.
>>   Research and evaluate similar events in other church-
es locally and nationally 5/1/87 to 9/1/87.
>>   Review progress with Governing Body monthly.
>>   Recommend broad plan including how to get entire
FCC involved in the planning and implementation
10/1/87.
>   Charge committees, organizations, and staff to use 1988
planning cycle for developing 1989–91 plans consistent
with 100th Anniversary vision, theme, and guidelines
2/1/88.

GB-3   Coordinate and execute process for electing, training, and in-
stalling FCC leaders.
>   Nominating Committee:
>>   Request specific qualifications (duties and respon-
sibilities) of candidates needed to fill 1987 vacancies
7/1/86 and 7/1/87.
>>   Assemble list of potential candidates with input from
the Membership Committee and congregation-at-
large 8/1/86 and 8/1/87.
>>   Conduct meeting to inform potential candidates
of opportunities to serve, duties, and time commitment.
>>   Determine their interest 9/1/86 and 9/1/87.
>>   Select candidates and verify their understanding
of responsibilities and required time commitment

10/1/86 and 10/1/87.

Present nominations and elect FCC leaders at duly stated Congregational Meeting 10/19/86 and 10/18/87.

Newly elected FCC leaders:

Participate in FCC Leadership Workshop conducted by CE and P&R 12/13/86 and 12/12/87.

Be observers at Nov./Dec. Governing Body meetings.

Governing Body Retreat planned by P&R 1/17/87 and 1/16/88.

Installation of FCC leaders 1/18/87 and 1/17/88.

GB-4   Appoint a taskforce to plan and implement an all-church celebration and recognition (high school seniors, college graduates, teachers, choir, *et al.*) banquet on May 14, 1987.

Appoint task force 11 /1/86.

Initiate planning 11/1/86.

Recommend to Governing Body 2/1/87.

Implement 5/14/87.

Evaluate 6/1/87.

GB-5   Coordinate auditing of FCC financial records and funds with Auditing Committee.

Review audit plan 11 /1/86 and 11 /1/87.

Receive audit report by 6/15/87 and 6/15/88.

Assure presentation to congregation by 6/30/87 and 6/30/88.

Membership

Mem–1   Document and implement process (roles of staff, committee, church members) for obtaining new members for FCC.

Advertise for new members twice per year in the Sunday Bulletin and Newsletter.

Periodically remind members to provide names of prospective members and to help in recruiting process.

Mem–2   Develop, implement, and continually evaluate effectiveness of an external communications plan 11/1/86.

Weekly ads in *Anywhere Journal.*

Ads in other papers (college, suburbs, etc.).

News releases to press, radio, TV, etc.

Other approaches.

Mem–3   Develop, implement, and continually evaluate effectiveness of internal communications plan for FCC members 11/1/86.

Weekly Sunday Bulletin.

Monthly Newsletter.

Other approaches.

Mem–4   Publish special pieces as appropriate.

Church brochure 10/1/86.

Stained glass symbology 3/11/87.

Mem–5   Expand fellowship groups.

College-age group

Make contacts starting 9/1/86.

If warranted, organize 2/1/87.

Adult fellowship groups

Evaluate and reorganize 10/1/86.

Mem–6   Evaluate needs and develop alternative means for ministering to special constituencies.

	Initiate Study	Recommend-tions
Campus	9/1/86	1/1/87
Singles	11/1/86	2/1/87
Denominationally-mixed marriages	2/1 /87	4/1/87
Adult men	6/1/87	8/1/87

Mem–7   Maintain and utilize Member Information Forms.

Obtain forms from all new members within two weeks.

Respond to committee requests for candidates within one week.

Suggest candidates to committees periodically.

Mem–8   Evaluate quality and level of membership participation.

Collective membership:

Develop evaluation criteria 12/1/86.

Evaluate, determine strengths and limitations, and inform Governing Body 5/1/87.

Individual Members:

Appoint sub-committee 9/1/86 and 9/1/87.

Assist Pastor in conducting role review 11/1/86 and
9/1/87.

Mission and Social Action

M&SA–1   Compile listing of current (1986) M&SA activities and related
human, material, and financial support.
Complete 8 /1/86.

M&SA–2   Develop and execute in concert with S&F plans for traditional
special offerings in support of M&SA.
One Great Hour of Sharing 3/22/87.
Christmas offering 12/7/86 and 12/6/87.

M&SA–3   Develop in concert with CE and S&F means for teaching and
promoting M&SA as an essential element in the spiritual lives
of individual members and of the congregation.
Complete plan 12/1/86.
Execute throughout 1987.
Evaluate quality of M&SA effort at FCC 9/1/87.

M&SA–4   Discover and/or create and evaluate new opportunities for FCC
leadership and/or participation in M&SA.
Initiate studies 8/1/86.
Progress report to Governing Body 2/1/87.
Integrate appropriate findings into 1988 planning.

M&SA–5   Develop a creative and aggressive 5-year M&SA plan requiring
at least 25% of FCC operational budget for M&SA activities.
Initiate studies 8/1/86.
Recommendations to Governing Body 4/1/87.
Integrate Governing Body approved M&SA recommen-
dations into 1988 plans.

Music and Worship

M&W–1   Increase youth involvement on Sunday mornings to at least 20
each week via:
One liturgist monthly
One usher weekly
Two greeters monthly
One on each communion clean-up
Three choir members

Youth oriented liturgies and music

Children's sermons monthly

Sunday morning baby sitters

Education for children and parents for children's communion.

Participation in church school

Regular church attendance

Youth talent

M&W–2   Develop in concert with Pastor, Director of Music, and M&SA, CE, S&F, and Membership Committees a 1987 calendar of Worship Service themes that emphasize in a timely way the activities and mission of FCC and integrate into worship service.

Initiate planning 9/1/86.

Inform Governing Body 12/1/86.

M&W–3   Sponsor an FCC member art and craft exhibit as a part of Sunday morning worship, church school, and coffee hour activities.

Initiate planning 11/1/86.

Implement 3/1/87.

M&W–4   Provide instruction and coaching for worship service liturgists.

Develop and implement plan 9/1/86.

Evaluate effectiveness Quarterly.

M&W–5   Develop a viable approach to mid-week Lenten worship services.

Initiate planning 8/1/86.

Recommend to Governing Body 10/1/86.

Implement 2/1/87.

M&W–6   Conceive, evaluate potential, and recommend implementation of at least one major new M&W activity for implementation in 1987.

Initiate study of activities such as bell choir, repeat of *Godspell,* stage a drama or musical, member talent show, liturgical dance, jazz service, performance and/or worship service by UFCCA Seminary personnel, spiritual life conference, etc. 8/1/86.

Recommend to Governing Body 2/1/87.

Implement in 1987.

Personnel

Per–1   Review and modify job descriptions for all paid staff (minister, DCE, organist, etc.) in concert with the minister, incumbent, and related committee or Governing Body.
> Initiate review 10/1/86 and 10/1/87.
> Complete 12/1/86 and 12/1/87.

Per–2   Develop work plans and performance goals for all paid staff in concert with incumbents, minister, and related committee or Governing Body.
> Initiate 11/1/86 and 11/1/87.
> Complete 12/31/86 and 12/31/87.

Per–3   Conduct and document performance evaluations of all paid staff in concert with incumbent, minister, and related committee or Governing Body.
> Semi-annually during March and September.

Per–4   Review salaries and make salary recommendations based on performance evaluations in concert with minister and related committee or Governing Body.
> Present recommendations to Governing Body 10/1/86 and 10/1/87.
> Inform and discuss with each paid staff member 10/8/86 and 10/8/87.

Per–5   Review and modify as appropriate the FCC compensation plan.
> Collect pertinent information annually during July.
> Complete review and make recommendations to Governing Body 9/1/86 and 9/1/87.
> Inform paid staff of any changes 9/8/86 and 9/8/87.

Plan and Review

P&R–1   Review FCC By-laws.
> Initiate 9/1/86.
> Recommend changes 11/11/86.

P&R–2   Prepare 1988 church calendar with inputs from staff, committees, and organizations.
> Request inputs 4/1/87.
> Receive inputs 7/1/87.

Publish and distribute 9/1/87.

P&R–3   Provide leadership, support, and integration for 1988 planning.

Obtain Governing Body approval of planning guidelines, planning calendar, mission, vision, etc. 2/11/87.

Receive 1988 committee objectives 5/1/87.

Obtain Governing Body approval of 1988 program plan to be used as a basis for resource planning 7/1/87.

Integrate and modify (if necessary) 1988 program plan and S&F resource plan for approval by Governing Body 10/1/87.

In concert with S&F present 1988 FCC Operational Plan to congregation 10/4/87.

P&R–4   Plan and implement Governing Body retreat.

Initiate planning 9/1/86 and 9/1/87.

Recommend to Governing Body 11/1/86 and 11/1/87.

Implement 1/17/87 and 1/16/88.

Stewardship and Finance Committee

S&F–1   Plan a more creative and interesting stewardship campaign that will draw the active interest and participation of the greatest possible number of church members.

Collect and study materials available from UFCCA and elsewhere to help S&F committee develop a better understanding of the totality of stewardship: time, talent, and gifts. Explore the use of expert resources from UFCCA headquarters or elsewhere. Complete 2/1/87.

Develop detailed stewardship plan, including interpretation, for 1987 and 1988 5/1/87.

Implement new stewardship approaches as soon as feasible (even before study and plan are completed).

S&F–2   Develop church resource plan for 1987 and 1988.

Request to committees and church staff for needed resources (financial and people) to implement operational plan approved by Governing Body at June meeting. 7/1/86 and 7/1/87.

Receive inputs from Committees and staff 8/15/86 and 8/15/87.

Prepare resource plan for preliminary review at August Governing Body and final approval at September Governing Body.

In concert with P&R (see P&R–3) present 1987 and 1988 FCC Plan to congregation 10/5/86 and 10/4/87.

S&F–3   Plan and conduct a stewardship campaign to meet the resource requirements (people and financial) of the 1987 and 1988 church plans.

Develop and implement plan 9/1/86 and 9/1/87.

Evaluate effectiveness 12/1/86 and 12/1/87.

S&F–4   Develop and execute plan for actively involving youth—all ages—in stewardship campaign and in giving.

Complete plan 8/1/86.

Implement 9/15/86.

Evaluate effectiveness 12/1/86.

S&F–5   Set increased goals for the special offerings, interpret needs and use to congregation, and attain the goals. Do this in concert with M&SA (see M&SA–2).

One Great Hour of Sharing 3/22/87.

Christmas offering 12/7/86 and 12/6/87.

S&F–6   Through a Memorials and Endowment Sub-committee, develop a church endowment fund. Encourage giving by church members to the Endowment Fund or the Memorial Fund.

Establish Endowment Fund 9/1/86.

Promote funds to congregation periodically.

Report status and use of funds at least annually.

Proposed 1987 *Resource Allocation*
Fictitious Christian Church—Anywhere, USA

The Governing Body of FCC estimates that the financial resources to support the expanded and more vigorous 1987 program for fulfilling the FCC mission as described herein will be $162,100, an 11% increase over the 1986 planned expenditures. The Governing Body is re-focusing the FCC program as follows:

Estimated Proportion of Total Expenditures

Program Element	1986	1987
Nurturing FCC members in worship and education	75%	65%
Helping members live and serve in the manner of Jesus	13%	20%
Telling the good news in Anywhere and throughout the world	12%	15%
	100%	100%

FCC has other special resource needs in 1987. In addition to the continuing dedicated service of many FCC members in a wide variety of FCC activities, there will be an urgent need for church school teachers. The CE Committee is planning some training sessions to help prepare people for this important service. The M&SA Committee has several unusual opportunities for FCC members to work with social agencies in the Anywhere area. FCC members have been blessed with financial, intellectual, time, and spiritual resources. The Governing Body asks you to consider prayerfully how you can use your resources to serve our Lord and Master in the fellowship of FCC.

A detailed line budget of estimated financial requirements for the 1987 FCC program is presented below.

Proposed 1987 *Income and Expense Budget*
Fictitious Christian Church—Anywhere, USA

Income

Source	1986	1987
Pledges	135,678	150,700
Plate offerings	2,300	2,500
Special offerings	5,200	6,000
Interest	2,500	2,500
TOTAL	$145,678	$161,700

Expenses

Item	1986	1987
Staff compensation	79,500	84,000
Office and administration	5,300	5,700
B&G	28,828	28,000
CE	2,900	3,500
GB	900	2,900
Mem	600	600
M&SA	23,450	32,500
M&W	3,000	3,600
Per	—	—
P&R	200	300
S&F	1,000	1,000
TOTAL	$145,678	$162,100

Note: Each of the line items shown above can be further sub-divided to show in however much detail the staff, Governing Body, and committees desire.

An Example of Committee Responsibilities in a Local Church

*An Example of Committee Responsibilities
in a Local Church*
Fictitious Christian Church—Anywhere, USA

1. There shall be eight committees of the Governing Body and two committees of the Congregation:

Governing Body
    Buildings and Grounds
    Christian Education
    Membership
    Mission and Social Action
    Music and Worship
    Personnel
    Plan and Review
    Stewardship and Finance
Congregation
    Auditing
    Nominating

2. The following rules shall apply to all Committees of the Governing Body:

A. Each shall have a minimum of two Governing Body members, one of whom the Governing Body shall appoint as Chairperson. Each shall also have a minimum of two members from the Congregation.

B. Each shall meet at a stated time and when called to meet by the Chairperson or the Governing Body.

C. Each shall elect or appoint a secretary to keep minutes, handle correspondence, and prepare a monthly report covering all work completed by or in progress within the Committee. The report shall be in the church office within two days following the Committee meeting. At the next Governing Body meeting the Chairperson or substitute shall present the report to the Governing Body.

D. The Governing Body is the ultimate authority. Committees may make recommendations, but approval of policies, program plans, and budgets rests with the Governing Body. Committees have authority for and are expected to make implementation decisions and take action within the policies, program plans, and budgets approved by the Governing Body.

E. Ministers of the church and staff shall be members *ex-officio* and without vote of all Committees.

F. Each shall prepare a program for the succeeding year to achieve its purposes and within the overall planning guidelines developed by the Governing Body. The planning year for each committee should be consistent with its mission (*e.g.*, the Christian Education Committee should plan its program for the "academic year" rather than the "calendar year"). These plans should be presented to the Plan and Review Committee no later than May 1st for integration into the overall church plan. The overall church plan shall be presented to the Governing Body by the Plan and Review Committee no later than July 1st.

G. Each shall prepare an annual budget to fulfill the Committee's plans and goals as set forth in the overall church plan approved by the Governing Body. The annual budget shall be presented to the Stewardship and Finance Committee no later than September 1st for integration into the total church budget for approval by October 1st.

H. Each shall be responsible for approving the payment of their bills within the approved budget and for monitoring and controlling committee expenditures.

3. The employed staff (*e.g.*, Staff Assistant / Director of Christian Ed-

ucation, organist, choir director, secretary-bookkeeper, custodian, *et al.*)
shall report to the Pastor as Head of Staff for administrative purposes. As
described in the following pages, Governing Body committees and staff
have a relationship for support and implementation as follows:

Staff	*Governing Body Committee*
Director of Christian Education	Christian Education
Organist	Music and Worship
Choir Director	Music and Worship
Secretary-bookkeeper	Personnel
Custodian	Buildings and Grounds

4. Governing Body and Congregation committee responsibilities are
described on the following pages.

Buildings and Grounds

Purpose: To support the Pastor and the Custodian in developing,
maintaining, and operating the buildings and grounds of Fictitious
Christian Church. The *ex officio* member is the Custodian.

Responsibilities:

- Provide for repair and maintenance of buildings and grounds.
- Provide insurance.
- Evaluate needs and opportunities and develop and implement one and five-year plan to provide building and grounds that support the total church program.
- Prepare one and five year operating and capital budgets for Buildings and Grounds.
- Approve payment of Buildings and Grounds bills and monitor and control expenses within approved budget.
- With guidance and assistance from the Personnel Committee, prepare job description for Custodian, recognizing the on-going supervisory relationship to the Pastor; develop

work plan and performance goals in concert with the Custodian and the Pastor; recommend salary actions to Personnel Committee based on performance evaluation against work plans and goals.

Christian Education

Purpose: To support the Pastor and the Director of Christian Education in the development and implementation of an educational program for Fictitious Christian Church.

Responsibilities:

- Evaluate, plan, and implement total educational program to meet the needs and opportunities for Fictitious Christian Church.
- Provide:
  - Learning opportunities for children, youth, and adults.
  - Confirmation and commissioning classes for communicants and new members.
  - Youth fellowship group.
  - Special ministries for older adults, parents, families, singles.
  - Continuing education events for church leaders and committee members.
- Examine and recommend or develop materials for teaching and learning.
- Provide appropriate learning environment for learning and teaching, including rooms and equipment.
- Recruit, train, and support teachers.
- Train and schedule nursery attendants.
- Inform congregation about educational needs, opportunities, and program.
- Prepare an annual budget for total educational program.
- Approve payment of Christian Education bills and monitor

and control expenditures within approved budget.

- With guidance and assistance from the Personnel Committee, prepare job description for Director of Christian Education, recognizing the leadership role of the D.C.E. for the educational program, the administrative relationship of the D.C.E. to the Pastor, and the supporting and implementation roles of the Christian Education Committee; develop D.C.E. work plans and performance goals in concert with the D.C.E. and the Pastor; make salary recommendations to Personnel Committee based on performance evaluation against work plans and goals.

Membership

Purpose: To support the Pastor and Director of Christian Education in enriching the church's ministry to its own members and in reaching out to all who may be seeking a relationship with Christ through Fictitious Christian Church.

Responsibilities:

- Maintain membership roles and pertinent demographic information.
- Visit, contact, and rejuvenate inactive members.
- Make newcomer contacts and visitations.
- Provide reception for communicants and new members.
- Organize fellowship groups (except youth) and provide resources and materials.
- Contact college students and provide programs for fellowship and affiliation while in Anywhere, USA.
- Organize coffee hour hosts from members within the Congregation.
- Develop a public relations ministry through radio, television, newspaper, newsletter, etc.

- Develop and implement a plan to fulfill the Committee purposes.
- Prepare an annual budget to support the plan.
- Approve payment of bills and monitor and control expenditures within approved budget.

Mission and Social Action

Purpose: To support the Pastor in developing, advocating, and implementing a mission and social action plan (local, national, worldwide) to fulfill the mission of Fictitious Christian Church.

Responsibilities:

- Be a source of information and knowledge about all mission and social action activities and opportunities sponsored by the UFCCA.
- Be a source of information and knowledge about Anywhere, USA, mission and social action activities and opportunities sponsored by FCC, other churches, community organizations, and government.
- Evaluate all mission and social action activities and recommend an appropriate role (spiritual, people, financial) for FCC.
- Initiate studies to discover and/or create new opportunities for FCC participation and leadership in mission and social actions in the Anywhere area and beyond.
- In concert with Christian Education, Membership, Stewardship and Finance, and the Pastor and Director of Christian Education, present a continuing array of speakers, worship services and sermons, promotional materials, projects, and events emphasizing mission and social action needs and opportunities.
- Advocate a growing mission and social action thrust for FCC, including a growing proportion of the operating

budget allocated to mission and social action activities. Fund raising, *per se,* is the responsibility of the Steward-ship and Finance Committee.

- Develop and implement a plan to continually enhance FCC's performance in the area of mission and social actions.
- Prepare a budget for Mission and Social Action.
- Approve payment for Mission and Social Action bills and monitor and control expenses within approved budget.

Music and Worship

Purpose: To support the Pastor, choir directors, and organists in developing and guiding the life of the church as it expresses itself in worship and music. *Ex officio* members are choir representative and Head Usher.

Responsibilities:

- Engage in study of worship; evaluate and recommend any changes in the order of worship.
- Provide and schedule in concert with the Pastor various types of worship opportunities (*e.g.,* traditional, informal, special observances).
- Guide and support the ministry of music at FCC.
- Provide printed materials on Christian worship as it pertains to policy in the following areas:
  - Sunday worship (bulletins and order of service)
  - Children's involvement
  - Sacraments of Baptism and Lord's Supper
  - Weddings and funeral services.
- Arrange for pastoral supply when needed.
- Recruit, train, and schedule liturgists, greeters, acolytes, and communion servers.

- Encourage and arrange ecumenical worship with other churches (*e.g.*, Lenten services).
- Arrange for flowers for worship services.
- Develop and implement a plan to fulfill the Committee purposes.
- Prepare an annual budget for Worship and Music expenses.
- Approve payment of Music and Worship bills and monitor and control expenses within approved budget.
- With guidance and assistance from the Personnel Committee, prepare job descriptions for choir directors and organists, recognizing their leadership roles for the music program, the administrative relationship to the Pastor, and the supporting and implementation roles of the Music and Worship Committee; develop work plans and performance goals in concert with choir directors, organists, and the Pastor; make salary recommendations to Personnel Committee based on performance evaluations against work plans and goals.

Personnel

Purpose: To develop and recommend personnel policies and practices to the Pastor, Governing Body, and Congregation. To guide and assist staff and Committees in carrying-out their personnel-related responsibilities. The membership is comprised of the Governing Body secretary and the Chairs for the Music and Worship, Christian Education, and the Buildings and Grounds Committees. When feasible, continuity in the Personnel Committee should be provided by appointing the Chair for successive years.

Responsibilities:

- Hire and terminate all lay employees.
- Develop generic approaches and format for job descrip-

tions, work plans and performance goals, and performance evaluations to be used by Committees with guidance and assistance from the Personnel Committee.

- Guide and assist the staff and the Committees in the preparation of job descriptions, work plans and performance goals, performance evaluations, and recommendations for salary actions.
- Review job descriptions to assure they are current and understood by the Governing Body, appropriate Committees, and the professional and support staffs.
- Implement staff performance appraisals at least semi-annually, salary reviews at least annually, work planning and goal setting at least semi-annually in concert with appropriate Session Committees.
- Review salary actions recommended by Committees and prepare an overall recommendation for salary actions by the Governing Body.
- Review personnel situations and actions when appropriate with the Congregation.
- Support and counsel staff in personnel matters.
- Prepare job description for secretary-bookkeeper, recognizing the on-going supervisory relationship to the Pastor; develop work plans and performance goals in concert with the secretary-bookkeeper and the Pastor; and recommend salary actions based on performance evaluation against work plans and goals.

Plan and Review

Purpose: To help enhance the short and long-range vision of Fictitious Christian Church leadership in developing, promulgating, and fulfilling the mission of FCC. To provide leadership and support to the Pastor, Governing Body, and Committees in developing, integrating, and reviewing Committee and overall church plans.

Responsibilities:

- Develop and implement a plan to fulfill the Committee purposes.
- Lead the Governing Body in developing, evaluating periodically, and modifying as appropriate the mission for FCC.
- Develop and distribute a summary of pertinent FCC, Anywhere area, and national environmental factors (demographic, economic, sociologic, etc.), planning guidelines, and planning calendar to the Governing Body and the Committees.
- Review, rationalize, and integrate committee plans into an overall church plan for presentation to the Governing Body no later than July 1st.
- Review progress of Governing Body and Committees against plans and goals and report status and recommendations at each meeting of Governing Body.
- Schedule and display calendar for church events and usage.
- Evaluate FCC by-laws periodically and recommend changes to the Governing Body and/or Congregation.
- Plan and conduct an annual Governing Body retreat.
- Prepare an annual budget to support the Plan and Review Committee plan.
- Approve payment of Plan and Review bills and monitor and control expenditures within approved budget.

Stewardship and Finance

Purpose: To support the Pastor in developing and implementing a total stewardship plan that effectively utilizes the spiritual, human, financial, and natural resources entrusted to individuals, Fictitious Christian Church and society as FCC strives to fulfill its mission.

Responsibilities:

- Develop means for developing FCC commitment to Christian stewardship (spiritual, intellectual, financial, physical).
- In concert with M&SA provide Minute-for-Mission and other special speakers for the church's work and mission.
- Develop a total church budget (operational and capital) based on the integrated inputs from Committees and on the overall church plan approved by the Governing Body.
- Develop and implement a total stewardship plan, including an annual financial stewardship program that will engage the enthusiastic support of the entire Congregation.
- Plan and implement capital fund drives.
- In concert with other committees plan and implement special offerings (*e.g.,* One Great Hour, Christmas, etc.).
- Appoint and provide guidance to a Committee on Memorials and Endowments.
- Manage the corporate and financial affairs of the church, including the supervision of investments, endowments, Memorial Fund, and Major Mission Fund.
- Encourage and record current payment of pledges and provide periodic reports to Congregation and individuals.
- Provide church financial reports monthly to the Governing Body and quarterly to the Congregation.
- Support Auditing Committee in its work and in reporting status to Governing Body and Congregation.

- Prepare budget for S&F.
- Approve payment of S&F and monitor and control expenses within approved budget.

Auditing Committee of the Congregation

Purpose: To verify the accuracy of financial record-keeping, report on the financial status, and make recommendations concerning the management of Fictitious Christian Church's financial resources.

Responsibilities:

- Conduct or otherwise arrange for an audit of FCC's financial records and funds annually or when requested by the Governing Body or the Congregation.
- Recommend changes in financial record-keeping procedures to the Governing Body as appropriate.
- Recommend changes in how financial resources are managed to the Governing Body as appropriate.

Nominating Committee of the Congregation

Purpose: To enlist members of the Congregation to serve the mission of the church as leaders of Fictitious Christian Church and as members of the Nominating Committee and of the Auditing Committee.

Responsibilities:

- Determine in concert with staffs and Committee chairs the specific qualifications of the leadership needed to achieve the specific and overall church goals in the approved church plans.
- Assemble a list of potential candidates for church leaders from the Congregation at large.
- Approach potential candidates in person, review the church structure and time requirements (perform work, training, ordination service, etc.), and receive their commitment to fulfill their responsibilities and time re-

quirements if they are nominated and elected.

- Select nominees from the potential candidates and present nominations of selected candidates to Congregation.

About the Author

During his thirty-six year career with the General Electric Company, Lindon (Lindy) E. Saline managed various technical and business operations and corporate staff functions, including GE's Management Development Institute. He has published over fifty technical, educational and professional development papers and monographs. Throughout his business career Lindy's activities and contributions have been recognized with awards from universities, professional societies, and national organizations.

Lindy has been elder and president of a Lutheran church, trustee and moderator of a Congregational church, and elder of a Presbyterian church. Since his retirement in 1984, he has been active as a volunteer in numerous organizations in the La Crosse, Wisconsin area including the Chamber of Commerce, Franciscan Health System, Viterbo University, University of Wisconsin–La Crosse, Chileda Habilitation Institute, La Crosse Community Foundation, First Presbyterian Church, the Catholic Deanery of La Crosse, and Rotary.